SILVERADO

SILVERADO

Neil Bush
and
the
Savings & Loan
Scandal

by Steven K. Wilmsen

National
Press
Books

Washington, D.C.

A KVK Communications Ltd. book.

First Edition

Library of Congress Cataloging-in-Publication Data

Wilmsen, Steven K., 1962-
Silverado: Neil Bush and the savings and loan scandal
by Steven K. Wilmsen
208 pages, 15 cm x. 23 cm
Includes index.
ISBN 0-915765-89-6
1. Silverado Bankings, Savings and Loan Association—History.
2. Savings and loans associations—Colorado—Denver—
Corrupt practices
3. Bush, Neil, 1955-
4. Presidents—United States—Children—Biography.
5. Real estate development—Colorado—Denver.
I. Title
HG2626.D395W55   1991
364.1'68'0978883—dc20   91-18486
CIP

PRINTED IN THE UNITED STATES OF AMERICA

Acknowledgments

Thanking all the people who helped put out this book would require another book. They know who they are: government regulators and lawyers, former Silverado employees, accountants, secretaries and, in some cases, people who simply happened to be flies on the wall. Many of them risked their jobs to talk to me. Other dredged up memories they preferred to forget. They provided me with depositions, diaries and interviews, without which this project would have been impossible. They talked to me for the simple reason that they felt some injustices had been done, and for that, I thank each one of them.

I've accrued an impossible debt to the people who suffered my long hours and subsequent temperment: Veronica, for her patience and support; Mike Rudeen, for his deft and unwavering eye; my colleagues at the *Denver Post*, for putting up with my absence. Thanks also to the *Post's* business editor, Henry Dubroff and Jeff Rundles, who is as responsible as anyone for my career.

Finally, thanks to Joel Joseph and National Press; to Peter Moore and *Playboy*; and to my parents, neither of whom will ever be president of the United States but nevertheless told me I was a good kid.

Author's Note

The events in this book were compiled largely from public records—legal depositions, congressional testimony, regulatory memoranda and various documents obtained through the federal Freedom of Information Act. There is, however, a significant amount of original reporting not verifiable by public record, in part because civil and criminal investigations of Silverado and other figures involved with the thrift are still pending. This reporting necessarily relies on the memories of sources. Recognizing that memories aren't perfect and that personal biases can alter even the best recollection, I verified facts with at least two sources. Where possible, facts were further checked in personal diaries and other written accounts. Dialogue was reconstructed in the same way, using public records of conversations, newspaper accounts and the recollection of sources. This book includes material from 50 interviews including six with Neil Bush, conducted mostly during the first nine months of 1990 before he stopped talking to the press.

Table of Contents

Preface

A Fellow Traveler

Neil Bush stood before the window of his office in downtown Denver, talking to his wife on the telephone and staring absently at swirls of mist that drifted off the streets 20 floors below. Reporters were beginning to arrive in a conference room down the hall, where he would shortly begin to wage what he called "my stiff battle with the feds." Federal thrift regulators had accused Neil of conflicts of interest that contributed to the billion dollar collapse of Denver's Silverado Banking Savings and Loan, where he had been a director. Rather than accept the relatively mild penalty of being prohibited from ever engaging in conflicts again, Neil chose to fight. He would prove his innocence in court, he declared, and be vindicated before the eyes of the nation.

He tucked the telephone under his chin, and remarked into it that it was cold for July. He spoke for a few more minutes, scheduling a weekend fishing trip and a tennis match for later in the evening and hung up. He sat down at the desk, jotted the appointments on a desk calendar, and returned his attention to an interviewer. "I'm going to get out front with this thing," he said, rocking back in his chair. "I've decided to fight and suffer the consequences. I'm going to extend an invitation to the American public to get the facts.

The regulators have missed the boat on this thing. Silverado was no different than any other well-respected savings and loan, and I acted in prudence in all matters, just like any other respected director would in my position."

His battle would go terribly wrong. In fact, the American public would see that Silverado *was* like other thrifts, and they would see that Neil was like other directors. But that was where Neil miscalculated. They didn't like what they saw. For nine months, Neil called press conferences and made public appearances to clear his name. Instead of winning hearts, he brought into America's living rooms the self-dealing, the greed and the wanton excesses that crumpled Silverado and hundreds of other savings and loans into a $500 billion pile of wreckage.

I had been covering Silverado for nearly two years in January 1990 when I discovered in corporate documents that two of Silverado's biggest borrowers—who happened to be two of Denver's wealthiest real estate developers—were Neil's business partners. At the time, the nation was just beginning to wake to the notion that savings and loan failures were part of a catastrophic financial phenomenon. Government pencil pushers furiously crossed out their last estimations of the bailout's cost and figured higher ones. It was becoming increasingly clear that blame lay not in faltering real estate markets throughout the Southwest United States but in fraud, deception and greed. By all accounts, thrift failures were part of a single event that deserved the catastrophic words assigned to it. Words like debacle, crisis and scandal.

But the startling revelations that came out of thrift failures almost daily didn't yet stir much passion. They were business stories with complicated and arcane twists. And fault for the crisis lay in so many directions that rage was diluted. The story of Neil's business partners and the government investigation of his conflicts of interest, however, changed all that. Phones rang off the hook at the *Denver Post* and other newspapers with the angry voices of taxpayers, who were learning they would pick up the tab for a scandal they'd done nothing to create. The blame assigned to Neil bordered at times on the ludicrous. One caller explained in a clear voice how the president's son had organized the entire savings and loan crisis from a concrete bunker in New Hampshire. People picketed Neil's country club house, screaming, "Give it back, Neil." Wanted posters with Neil's face were plastered across the country. *Business Week* proclaimed: "The savings and loan crisis acquires a name and a face."

Neil appeared before the House Committee on Banking and Urban Affairs, where he admitted that some of his dealings were "a little fishy." In press conferences, he lashed out at his critics and said "self-serving regulators" were out to get him because of his name. His claim was partially true. Democrats made political hay of Neil's plight. Yet there was more to it than that. There was something about him that reached into the guts of the nation and squeezed. Standing before the nation, shaking his finger in utter indignation, Neil was the very ethos of the savings and loan crisis. He cut through all the daisy chains and the deregulation and the accounting rules to the quick of it. He believed it was his right to live on unearned wealth, that money was his right as long as it was there for the taking. Never mind that taxpayers would have to pick up the tab. In that respect he was like the hundreds of faceless thrift executives, accountants, lawyers, politicians and professionals of every stripe who caused, encouraged or allowed the crisis to happen.

Neil's story—of his unrestrained drive for position, money and social importance in Denver—is the tale of the thrift crisis itself. What lies before the reader is the story of the nation's quintessential thrift failure, of how Neil Bush and the forces of financial reform, wealth and greed converged in Denver like they did in scores of other American cities.

Part I

1

Babylon's Little Brother

The year was 1985. A long line of limousines and Rolls Royces moved along a driveway, each pausing to empty its passengers—Henry Kissinger from one, Sammy Davis Jr. from another, Frank Sinatra, Gerald Ford, Lucille Ball. In tuxedos and ball gowns, minked and sabled against the autumn air, nearly a thousand guests poured from the glittering automobiles, waving and smiling gaily for the paparazzi before entering what the New York Times called the biggest party in the nation. Forbes called it the wealthiest. Town and Country said it was the most important.

The less-recognizable guests presented at the door enormous pink invitations, folded so that the elaborately sculpted figure of a horse popped up when they were opened. The guests had paid $2,000 for the privilege of receiving the invitations. Hostesses offered them party favors—perfume, chocolate, Turkish hand towels—and they moved into a cavernous hall bathed in pink light, which emanated from a huge carousel suspended from the ceiling.

Presently, a 350-pound man with rosy cheeks, an extra chin and bright, piercing eyes, stepped to a lectern. He was the host of the affair. He was also one of the richest men in the country. A polite silence rippled through the hall as he began to speak. Raising his glass in a toast and opening his arms wide, his voice boomed. "Ladies and gentlemen," he said, "welcome to Denver."

The words, spoken by Denver oil billionaire Marvin Davis, reverberated with a meaning most of the guests that night could not possibly have imagined. If cities had souls that could speak, it would have been Denver's voice that echoed across the sea of upturned faces, proclaiming that it had finally become the city it was always meant to be—rich, important, the center of the universe, with the world at its feet. A businessman—a Denver businessman—stood on the dais above some of the most important and wealthiest people in the free world and welcomed them to his city. In New York or Washington or Los Angeles, such an event might have passed without meaning. But in Denver, it was the fulfillment of a destiny. For the better part of five decades, Denver had been the jealous little brother of the great metropolises on either coast. It was a provincial cow town in the eyes of the world, a nice place to raise a family, but the roads to success led to the East and the West.

Not anymore. Denver was rich, unimaginably rich. People made fortunes, sometimes in a matter of days. A fever possessed the city, unseen since the cold waters of the South Platte River had yielded a few glittering nuggets of yellow metal more than a century before. Tales of riches echoed across the plains, and people came flocking. It seemed that everyone was rich. "Oh, the youth," a society columnist gushed. "To see that many young, beautiful people with just barrels of cash—it was a wonderful sight."

Barrels wasn't the half of it. Money was everywhere, and making it in great quantities was surpassed in importance only by spending it. For an entire class of overnight-rich, there was a new barometer of status whose gauge registered only when money flowed; the more money spent, the higher the mercury climbed.

One oil baron built an eighteen-hole miniature golf course in his house, reportedly because his daughter didn't want to wait in line at a public facility. Real estate developer Richard Rossmiller installed an elevator in his home to take him to the wine cellar in the basement. "That time was like nothing you'll ever believe sitting here now," said Charles Hull, a banker at Denver's Colorado National Bankshares. "It was the Roaring '20s. Every other car on the street was a Mercedes. Everyone had a Mercedes. There was money to burn everywhere."

A certain part of Denver delighted in the orgy. It was confirmation to some that they lived in a real city; no backwater town could support that kind of depravity. To document it all, Denver publisher Bob Titsch founded a slick society magazine, ElectriCity. To launch his publication, he threw a giant party at the haute Fairmont Hotel, importing guests from New York, Los Angeles and Paris, including a dozen or so heirs to various European thrones. So what if he had to pay them to come? They were there, weren't they? One guest observed: "This shows Denver could be a well-dressed city."

Perhaps the strongest confirmation of Denver's new greatness came on January 12, 1981, when credits rolled for the first episode of "Dynasty," the prime-time TV soap opera. In the opening scenes, the camera panned Denver's newly constructed skyline, then swept across magnificent mansions, with courtyards and swimming pools cut into hilltops and surrounded by lush forests. Most viewers had no way of knowing that the mansions had actually been filmed in Los Angeles. The important thing was that "Dynasty" oil billionaire Blake Carrington lived in Denver, where he operated his empire from a 48-room mansion amid all the deceit, sex, power and unspeakable wealth any real city could want.

It was just a TV show, of course, but it represented Denver's passage into a new era. "That was the beginning," recalled Hull, the banker. "As ridiculous as it sounds, people identified with that show, and whether or not it's a coincidence, we were a changed city after that."

Oil in the late 1970s and early '80s was to Denver what gold had been in 1858. Word of the first gold strike had blazed east across the plains like a prairie fire. Some estimates say 150,000 Easterners, ne'er-do-wells and get-rich-quickers flocked to Denver. Many of them got rich, to be sure, but as often as the metal itself made fortunes, the very fable of wealth also begot money.

Opportunists found that they could make more money with less work exploiting the needs and dreams of gold-baron hopefuls than they could putting their picks into the earth. They staked worthless claims, then peddled them to the newcomers arriving almost daily. Landowners waited for the green grass of spring to sell their normally parched farms to gullible settlers. Gambling halls, of which there were more than any other kind of establishment, regularly relieved miners of the ore they had labored to find. Real estate developers bought land in great parcels, then sold it when the burgeoning town needed room for saloons, hotels and houses.

People found any way they could to make money, and house fires became a common occurrence as homeowners set their homes ablaze for the insurance money. It was a city besieged with greed. "The 'almighty dollar' is the true divinity," a pioneer named Isabella Bird wrote of the time. "And its worship is universal."

Finally, however, the gold ran out, and so did the people who dug for it. Suffering from what Mark Twain called the "Californian sudden-riches disease," they left for more fruitful claims. Along with them went the opportunists who had lived off them, leaving behind a more sedate population that set about making Denver morally respectable.

The city faded to little more than a muddy spot on the map where travelers stopped on the way to bigger and better places—Dallas, San Diego, Los Angeles, even Kansas City. It was humiliating for some, and it brewed a festering spot in Denver's soul that made it want to be bigger and better than ever before. In spasmodic attempts to restore Denver's stature, business leaders plotted futile schemes, such as proposals from the Chamber of Commerce in 1946 that Denver be made the nation's capital and be designated the United Nations headquarters. But such plans never materialized, and Denver slumbered in relative obscurity.

In the years following World War II, the city grew. But it was a sleepy growth, fed mostly by people who fell in love with the climate. The gambling fever of the gold days was smothered beneath great blankets of suburbs that middle-class families spread across the rolling hills at the feet of the Rocky Mountains. Indeed, speculation was abhorred by the dozen or so old-money families in Denver who controlled the city's purse strings. They were the families who had started Denver's first banks and investment houses. "We made the prairie bloom," boasted Claude Boettcher, founder of Boettcher & Co. Inc., Denver's oldest home-based investment bank. "We turned sagebrush into sugar beets." They held themselves up as patriarchs of the city, patriarchs who didn't care for expansion or spending.

So while other cities grew, Denver's old families refused to finance new ventures. Too risky, they said prudently. Banker William Gray Evans, president of First National Bank until 1959, issued this maxim: "At all times, be ready to pay off the depositors. No bank is sound unless it is completely, absolutely, and beyond all doubt in the black." Put another way by Merriam Berger, another old-guard Denver banker, "New shoes do not impress me so much as old ones well cared for."

These families held their white-knuckled grasp on the city into the 1970s, when rising oil prices reawakened Denver's money fever. The old guard's reign began to crumble. There were too few of them and too many others moving in. They barricaded themselves in old-money neighborhoods like the Country Club and the Polo Club grounds, where they held their parties politely and tastefully and exclusively among themselves. "There was plenty of money in Denver," a society maven said, "but it never left the drawing room." They intermarried to protect their blood and their fortunes from dilution, earning the Denver Country Club the nickname Denver Cousins Club. And they began to gray and die off, sometimes with a little help. Eighty-five-year-old James Dikeou, for instance, whose father had brought him from Greece and helped parlay a popcorn stand into a billion-dollar real estate empire, was bludgeoned to death in 1977 by a fifteen-year-old prostitute whom Dikeou regularly paid $5 for oral sex. The old families continued to work behind the scenes, continued to be rich, but the reigns of control were about to be wrenched from their fists.

The wrenching was done halfway around the world on the sands of the Middle Eastern oil-producing countries. OPEC price fixing sent crude prices rocketing from $2.25 a barrel to $12 before shooting to $36 when revolution broke out in Iran. Rich wells in the northeastern Colorado plains and the Western Slope of the Rockies began to make money as though cash itself were being sucked from the earth. It made Marvin Davis a billionaire in a matter of a few years.

Oil wildcatters, engineers, geologists and people who knew only that Denver's streets were paved with gold packed their bags and headed to Colorado. The words "economic boom" and "go-go years" can't contain the enormity of what happened. Not only did ever-climbing oil prices touch off an explosion of oil exploration; Wall Street, which perceives Colorado as an energy center during oil crises, shipped capital to the Rocky Mountains as if there were no tomorrow. Oil was just the tip of a giant economic pyramid. For every oil prospector who came to the state, more came to build houses, sell clothes, cook food. And just as greed made fortunes in the 1860s, so it did in the 1980s. Meyer Blinder built one of the nation's largest stock brokerage firms peddling penny stocks with the promise of getting rich quick. And investors lost millions in a scheme to extract gold flakes from wood chips.

The city's population grew so fast that demographers and economists couldn't keep up. Home builders doubled, tripled, quadrupled their business, creating more jobs and more tales of wealth that echoed across the land, bringing more people. New condo parks and subdivisions sprang from the Colorado dust virtually every week, and they sold so fast that buyers camped overnight at sales offices. "People were doing enormous second mortgages on their homes because property values were going up so fast you couldn't lose," said Hull, the banker. (One house that cost $37,190 in 1975 went for $85,242 in 1981.) Bankers were lending money like crazy. We thought values would go up forever. Nobody could see an end in sight. There was this feeling that Denver had finally become a real city."

Up from Denver's razor stubble of a downtown sprouted huge construction cranes—scores of them—that erected great concrete and steel monstrosities. "Never in my life have I seen so many construction cranes," another Denver banker said. "They were everywhere, all across the horizon. It was eerie. Like a flock of giant birds roosting." By 1981, the amount of office space in downtown Denver had exploded to nearly ten times the total a couple of decades earlier. At its completion in 1983, a single building, the fifty-six-story Republic Plaza, would contain more office space than all of downtown in 1950. Dominating the new skyline was a 697-foot pillar of red granite whose silhouette, the shape of a giant cash register, could be seen for miles.

In the shadow of these skyscrapers, in the midst of the suburbs, was a tiny thrift called Mile High Savings and Loan. Mile High was left behind in the great scramble for money, humbly doing business as it had since it was founded in 1957. But one of the prospectors who came to Denver in 1979, a young savings and loan executive named Michael Wise, would make the thrift one of the largest in the state. Who knows if cities are haunted by ghosts of the past? If they are, the words of Denver historian Thomas Noel are particularly prescient to the decade upon which our tale embarks: "The biggest buildings in Denver were always gambling halls."

2

The Pied Piper

In 1979, Mile High needed a new president. W. James Metz, a Denver investor, had bought the thrift in 1976 and installed a man from his mortgage banking business to head it. Two years later, the new president was caught skimming money from the institution, and federal thrift regulators forced him out. Metz needed a new man.

Regulators suggested Michael Wise, a dapper executive from the central plains of Kansas who, despite his small-town roots, "could charm the birds out of the trees" and was reputed to be one of the quickest brains in the business. So, in the spring of that year, Wise flew to Denver and had lunch with one of Mile High's directors, an affable, wealthy car dealer named Florian Barth.

Over lunch, Barth studied the young man who sat before him and listened for faults, character flaws. He didn't find any. Wise spoke slowly and deliberately, his words the texture of cream. His voice—clear and low, like it was being produced instead of spoken—was hypnotic, assuring. His black-marble eyes focused in conviction when he spoke. Thoughts emerged from his lips like prepared text, never a wasted word or stammer. When he moved, it was with economy and purpose. He walked with noiseless fluidity, like smoke, and his vision seemed to arc so that he looked down upon even taller people. An extraordinary man, Barth thought to himself.

Indeed, Wise seemed more than merely human. A protective aura hovered about him, shielding him from the elements that wrinkle the shirts and muss the hair of the rest of humanity. His expensive suits retained a perpetual razor crease, and the part in his luxuriant hair was as thin and straight as the edge of a sheet of paper. Wise's dazzling appearance impressed everyone he met, even high-flying real estate developers who prided themselves on their expensive clothes. "My God, the suits he wore," one developer said. "I remember thinking to myself, 'Bankers don't dress that well.'" Wise was fastidious in grooming his image, calculating the accouterments that put him in the best light. He confided to a friend once that he refused to allow aids to install a phone in his Mercedes because "people would think I'm in real estate."

The gilded veneer concealed a fervent desire to succeed. "He was driven like no one you'll ever see," a friend said. "He wanted the biggest and the best, and nothing was going to stand in the way. A lot of people didn't see that because he always looked so smooth and in control. He never lost his temper. It was a calculating, one-step-at-a-time drive."

Barth was nothing but impressed. By the time lunch was through, he felt sure Wise was one of the brightest, purest minds he had ever encountered. Ten years later—after Wise had become known as the architect of one of the nation's most infamous savings and loan failures—Barth remembered him this way: "He was a fine gentleman. Very bright. The guy doesn't have a crooked bone in his body. There were a lot of high rollers in this town, getting into messes in Las Vegas and everything. Not Mike. Mike just has to be one of the brightest guys around. He was the kind of guy who always looks good."

That was the secret. Even when the fires of disaster raged around him, Wise looked like a million bucks. He was a salesman like Willy Loman in Arthur Miller's play, and like

Willy he rode on a shoe shine and a smile. But Wise had more: He had the magic. He was a pied piper who could win loyalty and keep it. With his slow, irrefutable logic, he disarmed even his most vitriolic opponents. Brian McCormally, a federal regulator who became Wise's nemesis as examiners closed in on Silverado, lay awake nights, staring at the ceiling for the two years he tracked the rogue thrift. "You could look up at the blue sky, and he'd look at you with that smile of his and say, 'No, it's black.' And for a minute, you'd believe him." Wise transfixed his employees, investors, politicians and federal regulators, and they followed him down the rosy path to ruin. "He was fucking mesmerizing," said a former Silverado marketing director. "He was everything you or I would ever want to be."

And he was everything Ronald Reagan dreamed of when he envisioned a deregulated America. There wasn't anything that the nation's tired nag of a financial industry couldn't do with men like Wise holding the whip, Reagan believed. The president wanted entrepreneurs, people who would sink their spurs into a business that had grown fat and complacent at the government's trough.

True to Reagan's vision, Wise seemed to have found the secret to profitability, even when other thrifts shriveled and died. He took a lazy, homespun institution with used curtains in the windows and turned it into a glass and steel powerhouse known across the country. There was nothing Denver's business community could do but look on in wonder. The powerful U.S. League of Savings Institutions, seeing what miracles he performed at Silverado, catapulted Wise into its upper echelons, where he virtually controlled the thrift industry's political agenda and helped chart the course for savings and loan activity across the country. Congressmen welcomed him, believing in his prophecies of a new and wonderful kind of savings and loan.

But in reality, Wise exemplified the hundreds of thrift executives who made personal fortunes gutting nearly a third of the nation's savings institutions with deceit and self-dealing. "In each case, we're finding one man, one dominant person, who led his board of directors down the wrong path," said Tony Adamski, chief of the FBI's financial crime unit. "One way or another, they made their boards believe that what they were doing was okay. Those boards became little more than rubber stamps for the whims of the chairman."

Still, Wise was different from the Charles Keatings and the David Pauls of the savings and loan crisis. Keating got favors for his Lincoln Savings by showering money on politicians and cursing regulators, whom he called stupid. David Paul, chairman of CenTrust Savings in Miami, forged a Harvard diploma and shouldered his way through regulatory barriers with sheer intimidation. But those methods were crude to Wise's way of thinking. He would never be so vulgar as to simply reach into his bank's vaults to pay for yachts, private jets and prostitutes, as others had. Wise paid himself millions, but he never amassed the ridiculous icons of wealth that became hallmarks of some thrift executives' careers. "You're all wrong if you think Mike was in it for the yachts and the parties," the friend said. "Don't get me wrong: He did all right for himself. But it was the power he was after. He was headed for the top of the pyramid."

The tools he used in his climb were the most sophisticated regulators had ever seen. His career and his wealth were built on labyrinthine deals that seemed to vanish into thin air when federal examiners tried to grasp them. Shortly before the House Banking Committee opened hearings on Silverado's failure, lawyers from the Office of Thrift Supervision produced a copy of their report on Lincoln Savings. "This will give you an idea of the complexity of the case we're dealing with here," a thrift office attorney told reporters. "This is the case against Lincoln," he said, brandishing a half-inch-thick sheaf of papers. He motioned to two assistants, who dumped four five-inch-thick volumes onto a table. "This is our case against Silverado." Silverado was the work of a mastermind. A mastermind who could peddle his wares.

There is a belief among the class of souls who call themselves salesmen that selling is a talent, not a science. Either
you have it or you don't—the magic power lets its possessor
sense a customer's doubts even before the customer does.
Without thinking, the true salesman can sooth and cajole,
then move in for the quick and painless kill. When the best
salesman does his deal, the prey always believes he is better
for it. The only way to acquire the magic, the belief goes, is
to be born with it. Wise was.

Wise came from a little town on the windswept plains of
central Kansas called Emporia. Emporia is a place where
people "grow up learning to do the right thing," a resident
made a point of telling me. "Contrary to what you might
want to believe, this is no hick town." True. Emporia
produced William Allen White, creator of the *Emporia
Gazette*, considered by many to be one of the greatest jour-
nalists and statesmen in American history. Over the years,
Emporia has had other claims to fame as well. There have
been a number of professional athletes (like John Lohmeyer,
a star with the Kansas City Chiefs until injuries forced him
out of football and into a marketing position at Silverado)
and a series of gruesome murders. Still, at 30,000 people, it's
hardly bright lights, big city. It has a main street that feels as
if it could be in Mayberry, and a couple of grain elevators
dominate the skyline.

Wise's parents raised hogs and cattle on a small farm
north of town. His father, Robert, worked for the county
government, was president of the county fair board and
helped out with 4-H in his spare time. They were a "solid
Midwestern family" that tried to breed good values—hard
work and civic duty—into their children, a family acquaintance said.

The oldest of four children, Mike was an unremarkable
child in most respects. But he had an extraordinary knack for
winning friends. The earliest memories of his acquaintances
always recount a herd of followers. By the time he entered
Roosevelt High School, he was immensely popular. His
classmates voted him president of his sophomore and senior

classes. He played football, track and basketball. People began to notice that the young man possessed a valuable commodity. "People on the team paid attention to Mike," said Ron Slaymaker, Mike's high school basketball coach. "He had a charisma, a spark that people respected. He was a pretty good athlete, but more than that, he was a leader. He could get the team going even when I couldn't." Wise set himself apart from other students, adopting a formal—some said arrogant—air of success that he nurtured as he got older. Instead of the letter jacket and blue jeans that many of his friends wore, Wise often went to school in a gray herringbone suit. It was the beginning of his reputation as a conspicuously good dresser. "My God, the suits he wore," a Denver real estate developer later recalled. "I remember thinking to myself, 'Bankers don't dress that well.' "

Emporia's town elders habitually scanned the ranks of their youth for promising young leaders. The city suffered a troubling exodus of talent. Those who were good at what they did got what they could out of the little city, then left. The town's aging leaders worried that without bright young people to fill their shoes, the town would soon fall into decay. Wise, who was known, liked and talked about all over town, was soon spotted and groomed as a sort of savior. "There was a general feeling among the Chamber of Commerce folks and the movers and shakers around town that Mike was a real leader. Here, finally, was a young, strong guy who was universally liked," said Ray Call, executive editor of the Gazette. "There was a great deal of disappointment when he left."

But for a time, at least, he fulfilled his early promise. In 1967, he graduated with a business degree from Kansas State Teachers College in Emporia, and soon afterward, he married a pretty, outgoing young girl named Paula Bruckner, daughter of a prominent Emporia businessman. Wise went to work as a salesman at his new father-in-law's ready-to-wear men's clothing store. His success in sales became legendary. "There was a magic about him," said John Kretsinger, who owns another clothing store in Emporia. "He had this special gift to captivate people and assure them things are going to be great."

He became so well known that two years later Joe Morris, president of Emporia's Columbia Building and Loan, approached Wise and offered him a job. Kretsinger remembered: "They hired him because he had this huge following. He had this great smile that made people like him. They trusted him and wanted to buy from him. That's what they were looking for."

Together, Wise and Paula quickly became viewed as Emporia's first couple. He rapidly worked his way up through Columbia's ranks, becoming treasurer and then director. Morris was so impressed with the performance of his young hire that he put Wise in charge of a new branch. It was Wise's show. He chose the site, oversaw completion of the branch, hired its employees. For a marketing campaign he assembled for the branch, the Savings Institutions Marketing Society of America awarded Wise its annual Marketing Award. If there had been any doubt before, the town elders knew now that they had their man. In November 1975, the Gazette ran a full-page spread on him. "The Community spotlight is on a young civic and business leader," the headline read. "Michael Wise is a young Emporia executive who has put his talents for leadership and organization to good use, both in the community and his profession," the story continued. Wise gazed benevolently from the accompanying photograph with his everything-is-going-to-be-all-right smile.

But some of Wise's success apparently wasn't his own. A coworker at Columbia recalled: "Mike had a way of achieving what he wanted through other people and then taking the credit. That's just how he operated. I don't like to say it, in a way, because he was always very good to me. I just saw what he did to some other people. He got people to do things for him. In that respect, I guess he was a good manager. It was weird. People wanted to do things for him. He liked to put on a good front. He liked to give the air that he was successful. He lived in nice houses, every hair was always in place. But there were some people he cheated, and I think they saw through the facade."

Nonetheless, Wise was heaped with civic awards and duties, eventually becoming president of the Chamber of Commerce. As Wise became more successful, he and Paula moved to successively larger and more prestigious homes. They finally settled in a quaint, colonial-style house near the Emporia Country Club. At the first snow of each year, they held a party. The city's elite came to their house to toast their town and their friendship. Life couldn't have appeared better for the Wises. Many people envied them their happiness and success.

But all was not happy. In a scandal that rocked the town, Paula left Wise for a young doctor. The Wises divorced, and Paula moved away from Emporia. Wise became restless. Denver's cash register beckoned, and in June 1979, with a recommendation from federal regulators, he took the job as president of Mile High, where he would use his magic on regulators, auditors, employees and politicians to transform the little Mile High Savings into a tower of prosperity.

Part II

The Scam

3

Mess to Miracle

When Michael Wise walked into Mile High Savings to assume its presidency in June 1979, the thrift looked and acted about like it had for the twenty-two years since it was founded. Most of its loans were in home mortgages, and its operations were run from a little blond-brick building with an electric sign out front and curtains skirting the plate glass windows. The front door opened onto a not-terribly-busy street corner in Littleton, Colorado, which was once a town in its own right but had become a suburb of Denver directly to the north. Some Formica desks and worn carpet were testimony to the institution's humble existence, and in most respects it contributed as much as any other thrift to the toaster-for-your-money folklore of American savings institutions. In an act of extravagance for the times, Mile High had in 1966 awarded a glass jug full of dimes to a beaming customer, Mrs. John Schuenemeyer, who had won the prize in a drawing.

Over the years, the thrift had grown slightly, mostly by merging with other institutions in the area. A dozen or so people worked there, including three tellers, a handful of loan officers and some administrators. "It was a friendly place," an employee said. "People were always nice, and we just did our job and did it well." For the most part, the thrift steadily made money, though not a lot of it, under the guidance of its owner, Franklin Burns. Burns was a slow, methodical man who worked hard at his job. "He never put pressure on anybody," another former employee said. "The only thing he cared about was doing things right."

Burns preferred to keep the thrift's money in home mortgages. But in 1977, Mile High lent money on a small ski resort project. The project failed, and Mile High was in danger of insolvency. So Burns reluctantly sold his thrift to Metz. Mile High's troubles went deeper than the bad ski resort loan, however. Much deeper. Mile High, like a third of the nation's thrifts, was squeezed in the vice of sudden economic changes it wasn't set up to handle and a flurry of ridiculously ill-conceived banking laws that attempted to compensate.

Up to that point, Mile High was the product of a government policy designed to protect an industry that had allied itself with the American Dream. That dream, of course, is the ability for average Americans to finance the purchase of their own home, an ideal that was planted deep in the American psyche early last century.

The ideal evolved from two distinct kinds of institutions: savings institutions and loan institutions. Both were founded more or less simultaneously by private groups. They weren't intended to make a profit so much as to promote the virtues of thriftiness (hence the nickname "thrift") among the working classes, who couldn't afford the more aristocratic commercial banks.

New York's first savings bank, for example, was chartered in 1819 by the Society for the Prevention of Pauperism. It took deposits of such "small sums of money as may be saved from earnings of tradesmen, mechanics, laborers, miners, servants and others." But it didn't make loans, putting the money instead in government securities and other investments that brought a small return but were considered safe. Loan institutions sprang from much the same principle, starting in Frankford, Pennsylvania, where thirty-seven people organized the Oxford Provident Building and Loan in 1831. Each member initially paid $5 for a share of the institution and then continued to pay $3 each month. There were no depositors and the association paid no interest. When the association had enough money for a $500 loan, it was auctioned to the highest bidder, who had to use the money to build or buy a home.

Eventually, the two ideas were put together, and savings and loans were born. They took deposits to promote savings and lent the money back out for middle-class Americans to buy houses. Before long, they were an integral part of the American landscape.

But they were still private. They didn't have deposit insurance or government regulation like their brethren the commercial banks, which had operated under the auspices of the Federal Reserve System since 1913. Thrifts thrived and failed at the whims of the economy. So when the Great Depression wiped out 1,700 of the nation's 12,000 thrifts, President Herbert Hoover brought the survivors under the protective skirts of the federal government.

For all intents and purposes, the thrift industry became a stepchild of the government with Hoover's signing of the Federal Home Loan Bank Act of 1932. Among other things, the law created a system of government banks to fund savings and loans that consisted of the Federal Home Loan Bank Board in Washington and twelve Federal Home Loan Banks in districts across the country.

Despite the new law, most people who had lived through the Depression weren't terribly enthusiastic about putting their money into any form of bank, not after $200 million in deposits had simply disappeared. So in 1934 President Franklin Delano Roosevelt instituted deposit insurance of $5,000 an account. Recognizing that the government's money was now at stake should these institutions fail, the law imposed strict government regulation of institutions so insured. "We do not wish to make the United States government liable for the mistakes and errors of individual banks and put a premium on unsound banking in the future," Roosevelt declared.

Largely financed by these new government-protected institutions, the American Dream flourished. Home ownership grew from 14 million in 1930 to more than 50 million by the late 1970s. Likewise, thrift assets grew from $9 billion to more than $600 billion over the same period. The new system worked beautifully. Failures were rare—almost unheard of—and even more rarely did a homeowner default on the loan for his house. And so life for savings and loans trundled happily along for almost 30 years until a many-clawed creature called inflation reared its head in the 1960s, and Congress began to tinker with the system.

Compared with what was to come a decade later, inflation in the 1960s was relatively mild and brief. But it was enough to send interest rates up, scaring lawmakers into thinking that the cheap home mortgage would perish if they didn't act. So they set a limit on what thrifts could pay in interest on savings accounts. The reasoning went that if S&Ls didn't have to pay much for deposits, they wouldn't have to charge much for loans.

The ceiling didn't cause any real problems until the middle and late 1970s when inflation revisited, this time bigger and nastier than most people in this country could remember. Lyndon Johnson had tried at once to pay for a war in Vietnam and to encourage economic growth at home by printing huge amounts of money, sending prices for just about everything soaring. Then, Richard Nixon unhinged the dollar from its firm anchor in the gold supply, letting the currency's value tumble around at the whim of investors. And, as though fortune and calamity must come in threes, oil producers in the Middle East decided they weren't getting enough money for the black ooze that bubbled from beneath their sands; crude prices, along with prices for just about everything else, skyrocketed.

Interest rates stayed down while the Federal Reserve continued to pump money into the economy. But in a rare Saturday press conference in 1979, Fed Chairman Paul Volcker announced he was turning off the spigot in a move meant to stack crushing weight on prices. Economists can drone for hours about the effect of Volcker's move, but the long and short of it for thrifts was that short-term interest rates climbed into the double digits overnight. The measly 5.5 percent savings and loans paid for deposits at the time was a joke. No one in his or her right mind would keep money in a savings account that paid so little when money could bring double-digit returns from new inventions like mutual funds. Thrifts lost deposits by the truckload.

Savings and loans had to do something to stem this tide. So, clothed in the noble ideals of their founders, they went to Washington and pleaded their case. The builders of the American Dream would wither and die if they couldn't pay more to bring back the deposits they so desperately needed. Congress agreed. Starting in 1977, it began pulling the nails from the interest rate ceiling on deposits put in place less than a decade before, and thrifts punched up higher and higher rates to entice savers.

Congress evidently forgot, however, that for a thrift to stay in business, it has to make more money from loans than it pays for deposits. While thrifts hiked up the interest they paid for savings, Congress froze at the old level the rate they could charge for loans. That was like forcing cobblers to buy expensive shoe leather while artificially keeping shoe prices lower than the cost of the materials used to make them. If you were a cobbler, you'd stop making shoes because you'd lose money if you tried to stay in business. If you were a savings and loan, you'd stop making loans. And that's what most thrifts did, losing their main source of income in the process.

But that wasn't the worst of it. Not only did they stop making new loans, they also lost money on the loans they already had. Original thrift regulation had specified that home mortgages be paid over thirty years. After decades of doing business that way, thrifts had great piles of thirty-year mortgages made in the days of stable (and low) interest rates. By the late '70s, those mortgages earned a pitiful dribble of interest income while thrifts paid magnificent sums just to keep deposits from walking out the door.

Like the rest of the thrift industry, Mile High was healthy in 1972, when interest rates were still relatively stable. That year, the nation's thrifts had a collective worth of $16.7 billion. By 1980, that figure had crashed to a negative $17.5 billion. Mile High, accordingly, was practically broke. Eighty-five percent of the industry, including Mile High, was losing money. But Wise didn't let that deter him in his quest to build his one-horse institution into a financial powerhouse. Soon after coming to Colorado, he vowed to a friend to make Mile High into the largest institution in the state. So two months after taking over, Wise moved Mile High from the suburbs to a brand-new seven-story building in Denver proper. "The old place wasn't exactly Mike's style," said Chuck Henning, a former Colorado savings and loan lobbyist. The new building wasn't a match for Denver's 17th Street financial big boys, but at least it was in the city and near enough to downtown to draw some attention.

When Wise took over Mile High, savings and loan executives still ranked on the social and political hierarchy at roughly the same level as dentists. Most people realized that thrift operators performed an important community service, and they were generally looked upon as solid citizens and good neighbors. But they were the sort of men (most of them were men) who wore green golf slacks in their off hours and talked in appropriately reverent tones about what many of them called "bidnis."

But Wise made it clear he wanted his institution to have nothing to do with that crowd. A name like Mile High Savings, however, would keep him there like a stick in mud. The name made his thrift sound as tired and useless as the industry itself. So he hired a Chicago consulting firm to come up with a new name. He wanted something that would drive a wedge between him and the simpletons in green pants, a name that would raise the flesh of those who beheld it. After a few unsuccessful tries, the consulting firm finally came up with Silverado. It was perfect. The very ring of it commanded respect, like the cold stare from a band of rough riders. The Western image was no accident, and Wise exploited it. When he discovered that the first Western film to be released in decades would be titled "Silverado," he made sure that his thrift was a corporate sponsor. The ensuing advertising campaign flooded airwaves and newspapers with the silhouetted images of tall-riding cowboys, glaring steely-eyed from under the brims of their hats. Come to "where the West begins . . . and the adventure never ends," the ads beckoned.

Those advertisements might as well have been help-wanted ads, for Wise needed a new breed of employee as well. It's a cliche that a company's success depends on the people who work for it, but it's true, and Wise knew it. He also knew that if he was to make Silverado into the kind of institution he wanted it to be, he needed people who would follow him to the edge and never question his orders. This presented a problem. Thrift employees, for the most part, are part of the broader species of bankers. And bankers are genetically incapable of the kind of thinking Wise wanted from his employees. Bankers evolved from the financial panics that preceded banking regulation in the 1930s, and every fiber of their being is designed to assure customers of the safety of their money. Bankers tend to ponder, to put their fingertips together and frown whenever events threaten to take them beyond the clearly demarcated boundaries of prudence. But Wise needed people who thrived on life outside the rules. Ass-kickers and name-takers.

So Wise set about creating a corporate culture that would bring him the kind of people he needed. And he did it with a very simple change. Instead of describing Silverado's business as banking—or worse, home financing—he called it "go-go banking." Most people wouldn't give a second thought to such semantics. But a traditional banker would recoil in horror. An ass-kicker, however, would see that to work at Silverado was to be on the adrenaline-pumping jagged edge of financial America. *Where adventure never ends.* Such was the reaction of one vice president who had been working in banking for several years in Denver when he saw his chance to work for Silverado. "When I met Mike, I was sold instantly. You have to understand: Silverado was where the action was. It wasn't a bank. Nobody wants to work for a bank, for God's sake. It was go-go banking. It was a roller-coaster ride. It was life in the fast lane, and you couldn't miss a beat. There were people standing in line to get a job at that place. I worked for two years, 90 hours a week, and I felt privileged to do it. I was part of the hottest institution in the country, and I loved every damn minute of it."

The fact that Silverado paid more than virtually any other similarly sized institution in the country didn't hurt in fostering loyalty. But there was more. "People at Silverado were hard workers," said an executive vice president who helped manage Silverado's lending operations. "They were legitimate people who were good at what they did, and they worked harder and did their jobs better than any other company I've worked for. People worked 80-hour weeks, and I worked on Christmas Day more than once. Money doesn't get you to work that hard. You've got to have leadership, someone who believes that what you're doing is important. Mike made everyone feel that way." A vice president recalled: "Every day I thought to myself, 'Wow, I'm a lucky son of a bitch.' This guy was so quick, so sharp, so . . . something. He would just blow you away."

Meanwhile, Silverado got a boost from Congress, which was getting down to the business of the first major piece of thrift deregulation, the Depository Institutions Deregulation and Monetary Control Act. The Federal Reserve's Economic Review called it "the most important piece of banking legislation since the 1930s." The bill removed completely the ceiling on deposit rates, which had been pried away in pieces since 1977.

Institutions across the country jacked up their savings rates, but Michael Wise did it faster than virtually anyone else. He directed his thrift to pay some of the highest rates in the state and eventually the highest rates in the country, sometimes a full point above those of other institutions. Other savings and loan operators watched in horror as he matched their increases and more. "Somebody ought to tell that guy that the prime rate is what you lend at, not what you pay," a disgusted Colorado thrift executive remarked at the time.

The same bill hiked deposit insurance from $40,000 to $100,000. Fueled by high rates and Uncle Sam's guarantee, torrents of deposits flooded Silverado, doubling to $240 million less than a year after Congress passed the legislation.

Flush with cash, Wise wanted to grow and grow fast. There are several ways to grow if you're a financial institution. You can make new loans faster than old ones retire, you can buy other people's loans or you can simply buy another institution. There is no faster route than the last. So Wise took it. He found a savings and loan called Security Savings in Colorado Springs, a town seventy miles south of Denver, that was up for sale. At $90 million in assets, Security was almost as big as Silverado, and regulators protested that it was far too large for Silverado to swallow, especially considering that Silverado's capital position was dangerously weak. Nonetheless, Wise bought it.

A few months later, a team of federal examiners returned to Silverado for a regularly scheduled checkup of the thrift's financial statements. They were dismayed to find that Silverado had quadrupled in size in just ten months since the last exam. As they waded through loan documents and financial statements, they discovered that the thrift was losing enormous amounts of money, despite the fact that it looked as though Silverado was improperly booking profits from loan fees. Bad loans had increased, and expenses for salaries and other costs were twice that of other savings and loans its size. Worse than anything, capital had plummeted to 2.46 percent of assets, less than half the 5 percent that federal regulations required.

In the banking world, capital means everything. It's the main barometer regulators use to judge an institution's health and the primary guard against sudden insolvency. Perhaps most important for Silverado, it's a measure of how fast an institution can grow.

The formula for calculating capital is absurdly complex. But boiled to its essentials, it's the difference between assets and liabilities. It should be noted that bankers see the world in a mirror image from the rest of us: Loans, which produce income, are assets; deposits, which the bank must ultimately return, are liabilities. Therefore, the more good loans a bank has compared with its level of deposits, the healthier it is and the more able to withstand adverse conditions.

Before deregulation, savings and loans were required to keep a capital reserve of not less than five percent of their assets in a cash reserve. That way, if unexpected losses began to pile up, the thrift would have plenty of cash to give depositors while it recovered and began to make profits again. Having less than five percent was grounds for closing a thrift. Silverado's capital level was so far below the legal requirement that examiners felt certain the thrift would fail to replenish it before the end of the year. Silverado's days appeared to be numbered.

Wise assured the examiners that he would bring the institution under control and that "balance sheet strength is Silverado's primary goal, not asset size." Silverado doubled in size the next year. Again regulators told Wise Silverado's capital was too low and he must slow down. And again he assured them the thrift would soon be rock solid through a policy of "continued profitability and monitoring of asset growth." The thrift doubled again the next year.

The regulators' warnings might eventually have caught up with Wise, and he would have been forced to shrink the institution. Instead, Silverado—along with a thousand other thrifts in similar condition—got some unexpected help from a man named Dick Pratt, whom Reagan appointed to the Federal Home Loan Bank Board in 1981. When Pratt took office as the nation's chief savings and loan regulator, the industry was so sick that a 5 percent capital reserve was the exception rather than the rule. If regulators had chosen to close every institution that didn't meet the requirement, nearly a third of the industry would have been wiped out. At that point, the government had a number of choices to make the industry well, but they all came down to letting the sick portion of the industry die while the government dealt with the fundamental problems that had put them into the tank to begin with. That didn't sit well with the U.S. League of Savings Institutions, which would have seen about a thousand of its dues-paying members disappear. It didn't sit well with the Federal Deposit Insurance Corp., which would have had to cover every account insured to $100,000. And it certainly didn't sit well with the Reagan administration, which had pledged to make America great again.

So Pratt came up with an easier solution. Rather than endure the suffering and eventual death of the gangrenous third of the nation's thrifts, he simply changed the rules. With a few pen strokes, he made the industry healthy again, literally overnight. One of his first moves was to lower the regulatory capital requirement to three percent. This was good news for Silverado, which suddenly came much closer to the legal requirement. But there was more. Under Pratt's new regulations, thrifts could count almost anything as capital. Instead of just cash, thrifts could include everything from real estate to something known as goodwill. Goodwill is known in the trade as an intangible asset, the perceived value of a thrift's name and reputation. To the nation's deposit insurance fund, which capital cushions were meant to protect, goodwill has as much value as a mayonnaise jar full of air. But now thrifts could put it on their books as though it were genuine coin of the realm. From the acquisition of Security, Silverado was allowed to immediately add $23 million in goodwill to its capital level. Without doing a thing, Silverado was healthy again and free to grow.

With a little more help from Pratt, Silverado started to show huge profits. This time, the help came in the form of changes in accounting rules. Before Pratt stepped in, thrifts were required to spread fees they collected for mortgages over the life of the loan. In other words, a thrift could only count $10 toward its bottom line in each of ten years for a loan that generated $100 in fees. In part, the rule was an incentive to consistently make good loans over a long period of time rather than hand out money simply to collect the fee. Normally, savings and loans make their money from the interest on loans. But 85 percent of the industry was losing money. So Pratt revoked the rule and allowed thrifts to book all the fees the moment the loan was made.

Suddenly there was every incentive to make loans, period—good or bad. Silverado went mad lending money. Loan officers handed out money wherever they could. They regularly invited other financial institutions and mortgage companies to send borrowers their way. They gave their loan forms to any mortgage company that would take them, not just in Colorado but across the country. In their enthusiasm, they closed deals without first getting credit histories or appraisals, and if borrowers didn't have cash to pay closing fees, Silverado let them write up an I.O.U. As far as Silverado was concerned, it was as good as gold. Often, the thrift gave borrowers more money than they asked for. Because fees are based on the amount of money borrowed, the bigger the loan, the bigger the fee. Here lay the roots of Silverado's $1 billion failure. "Stripped to its essentials, Silverado's problem was that it primarily relied upon high-cost borrowings and lent money to people who couldn't pay back the money, period," said Brian McCormally, testifying before the House Banking Committee.

It was a feeding frenzy. But the frenzy was restricted to a relatively narrow spectrum of investments until 1982 because thrifts still had to keep the bulk of their assets in home mortgages. Reagan changed that on October 15, 1982, when he walked into the Rose Garden at the White House and signed the Garn-St. Germain Act of 1982, the hallmark of his administration's financial deregulation. Two hundred savings and loan executives, bankers and congressmen beamed as he signed away fifty years of thrift regulation and opened the door for investments in commercial real estate and other investments that before were seen as too dangerous for thrifts.

Silverado's floodgates opened. No longer did it have to rely on home mortgages for its growth. Raw land, office buildings, shopping malls—that was the ticket now. The loan portfolio grew exponentially, rocketing 800 percent from 1982 to 1986. Silverado became the fastest-growing thrift in Colorado and one of the fastest-growing 10 percent in the country.

New deals came in so fast that the staff couldn't keep up. Records were sloppy and often nonexistent. Sometimes staffers put together loan documentation after the deals were done. "We were growing so fast that I'd have to check every couple of days to see where our assets were," Silverado's marketing director recalled. "I'd write press releases for one thing or another and if we delayed it for a couple days, I'd have to revise it with new asset figures."

Silverado appeared to be on easy street. The loans themselves may not have been making much money for the thrift. In fact, many of them went bad within months of being made. But it didn't matter. Denver's economy was booming. Real estate developers climbed over each other to get money for vacant property and to build offices, strip malls and condos. The demand for money was exceeded only by the rate at which real estate values climbed. So what if Silverado lent more money for a parcel of ground than it was worth? In a year or even a couple of months, it would probably be worth more. And so what if loans went bad? Silverado could afford to chuck bad loans into a closet like used furniture; for every loan that went bad, it made ten new ones, using the fees to make up for losses on souring loans. Before Pratt changed the rules of the game, Silverado had made only meager profits. In the first half of 1981, just before the change, it lost $1 million. But in the second half of the year, profits shot up to $1.5 million. By 1983, fees made up an astonishing one-third of Silverado's operating income.

In June 1983, Wise announced that Silverado would be moving again, this time to a 157,000-square-foot, thirteen-story glass tower southeast of downtown. Wise tried to wriggle out of a ten-year lease on the old building, but the owners wouldn't relent. Silverado ended up using the building as storage for supplies and furniture discarded from various offices, which were constantly being remodeled. Despite the old lease, Wise insisted that Silverado move. Space wasn't the issue. Rather, it was status. Wise had grown to disdain the seven-story building as he had the little street-corner shop four years before. After all, a thrift executive on his way to forming the largest institution in the state couldn't carry much weight in the corner office of a seven- story building.

The crown of the new tower was a palatial, marble-halled suite called the Skydeck. The Skydeck was accessible only by a staircase from the penthouse floor below and a private elevator restricted to Wise and a close circle of associates. Most of the thrift's executives had their offices in the penthouse, which hummed with the white noise of activity. On the Skydeck, Silverado's world became a different place. Sumptuous carpet lay in islands between marble walkways. The atmosphere was monastically silent and viscous with importance.

There were two offices on the Skydeck. One belonged to vice chairman Rick Vandapool, an imp-faced man and a loudmouth, at least compared with Wise. "He was supposed to be the people person. He was the guy that rubbed elbows with everyone," said an executive vice president. Vandapool sang out loud in his office and shouted to his secretary through the door, which he always kept open, interrupting the heavy quietness of the Skydeck. Stacks of paper and computer printouts sprawled across his desk in tumbling piles.

Wise's office was on the opposite end of the Skydeck, just out of shouting range of Vandapool's. Stepping over the threshold of Wise's office was like stepping out of one world and into another. Contrasting with the marble outside, the office was warm and wooden—oak floors and paneling, a magnificent Louis XIV desk with bookshelves behind and delicately upholstered antique chairs before it, placed as to suggest that a visitor might sit, but only if invited. In every respect, it looked as though it were not an office at all but the preserved study of some ancient patriarch with a new building erected around it.

There, Wise worked in long hours of silence, the door always closed, always wearing his suit jacket, sitting erect and plying himself to the paper before him. Invariably, it was the only paper on his desk. When he was through, he disposed of it and began to work on another, turning the pages over to form a neat stack. The sundry other items on his desk were arranged in Palladian symmetry. If they were inadvertently moved, he rearranged them before leaving his office and cleared the desk of anything that detracted from the order.

As a sign of the kind of institution Silverado had become, the lobby of the new building was finished in black marble and oak, with recessed lighting and the blue and silver of the thrift's corporate colors, all designed to distinguish Silverado to what management called "the high-balance customer."

High-balance customers—a banker's euphemism for rich people—were to become Silverado's meat and potatoes under the direction of Bob Lewis, whom Wise hired in 1984 to be his chief financial officer. Before coming to Silverado, Lewis had been a partner at a Big Eight accounting firm in Denver. He was a technician, a financial genius whom some of his co-workers called The Wizard. He perceived numbers the way an artist perceives colors; he could mix them, spread them around on the canvas of a balance sheet to create illusions of depth and shadow.

Lewis was to engineer a complete transformation of Silverado. He would move the thrift further and further from the original intention of savings and loans and concoct financial manipulations that would make Silverado known to thrift executives across the country. He believed that the thrifts of the past, the ones that catered to ordinary savers and ordinary home buyers, would perish. The only way to prosper, he thought, was to forsake that business. So he did.

Beginning late in 1984, he steered Silverado away from people with average incomes in favor of high-balance customers. Anyone who had at least $10,000 to sink into a certificate of deposit was welcome in Silverado's oak-finished lobby. But if you wanted to put away a few dollars a month for your kids' education, Silverado didn't want to talk to you.

Lewis preferred, in fact, that Silverado not deal with individual depositors at all. He reasoned that maintaining savings accounts costs money to pay tellers, accountants, data processors, leases for branch offices and so on. He also reasoned that millions of dollars in deposits were floating across the nation in search of the highest interest rate. Big investment banking firms, in fact, had scattered brokers across the land to ferry $100,000 bundles of investors' money toward the highest return from savings and loans. It was a booming business because thrifts were paying enormous rates, and by moving money around every day as rates at individual institutions undulated, they could make a killing. What's more, the investment was totally safe. The government guaranteed the safety of every penny as long as the bundle didn't exceed the $100,000 deposit insurance limit.

Brokered deposits, as they are called, were the darling of Reagan's economic advisers, who believed the invisible hand of the free market would nudge these mountains of cash to the thrifts who deserved them most. The healthiest thrifts could afford to pay the highest rates, so the thinking went. The thinking turned out to be disastrously wrong. In any event, Silverado hired brokers to scour the nation for these massive bundles of money. By cutting the expense of maintaining small accounts, Silverado could afford to pay higher interest rates, making the brokers' jobs that much easier.

Silverado's Money Desk was born. Like Wall Street traders, Money Desk brokers spent their days cold-calling money brokers and wealthy investors across the country to sell Silverado's latest interest rate, which changed daily. "We found that a half a point could move a hell of a lot of money from the little old ladies with shopping bags," one former employee said. Propelled by the commissions they got each time a big block of money moved, the brokers had pulled in 20 percent of Silverado's total deposit base by 1985.

Following the same thinking, Silverado shut down its loan origination offices late in 1984. Making loans, especially home loans, was expensive for the same reasons that keeping small savings accounts was expensive. There just wasn't enough money to be made on one of those deals, Lewis reasoned. Instead, Silverado could buy huge blocks of loans disgorged by other thrifts.

Congress had realized in 1981 that the piles of thirty-year mortgages warehoused by thrifts were nothing but a drain on the industry. So it devised a tax break to take care of the problem. It allowed thrifts to sell their mortgage loans and put their cash to work in more lucrative investments. Wall Street was ready for this development. In fact, some have argued that Wall Street lobbyists were responsible for convincing Congress of the wisdom of its legislation. Since 1977, when two traders at Salomon Brothers convinced Bank of America to sell its home mortgages in the form of bonds, big New York investment houses had bought thrift mortgages, pooled them together, sliced them into pieces and resold them like bonds. But the practice was legal only in a few states, and the business was small. But when Congress passed the 1981 tax break, it seemed as if every thrift in the country wanted to sell its mortgages to New York traders. More often than not, they used the money from the sale to buy loans disgorged from other savings and loans. The thrifts simply traded loan portfolios among themselves, selling them at 65 cents on the dollar when they had made them for 100 cents. Selling their loans at a loss was partly a reaction to the high short- term interest rates, which made the loans on their books a drain on income.

Wall Street firms did a booming business by the early 1980s, acting as middlemen for thrifts desperate to rid themselves of long-term mortgages and just as desperate to reinvest idle deposits. Wall Street traded the paper furiously, scouring the country for savings and loans who wanted to get in on the game. Silverado was one of them. At the end of June 1982, its portfolio included just $3 million of these investments. Six months later, that number had increased eight times to $24 million.

On January 25, 1985, Silverado reached $1 billion in assets. Wise was ecstatic. He ordered thousands of buttons and key chains that read "Thanks a billion! 1/25/85" for his employees and customers.

Silverado seemed the model of ruddy health envisioned by deregulation's proponents, and to those people Wise held the grail of prosperity. With it he won the hearts of Denver's business leaders, becoming treasurer of the Greater Denver Chamber of Commerce and a member of the University of Denver's Board of Fellows and a host of civic organizations. He wrote columns for a Denver newspaper and was one of the most frequently requested speakers at business functions in Denver and across the country.

Savings and loan executives from across the land came to hear him expound on the wisdom of his methods. Wise's speech writer recalled watching the effect Wise had on his audiences: "He was the kind of leader who could inspire. Mike had a . . . charisma, that's the only word I can think of. When he stepped up to a podium, you could literally see silence ripple through the audience. It was like he was Christ on the mount to these people. They wanted to hear what he had to say. You couldn't help but be attracted to him." Many thrifts around the country, hearing his words, later adopted Silverado's tactics.

Wise had listeners in Washington as well. His success at Silverado had catapulted him to the top of the powerful U.S. League of Savings Institutions. Despite its somewhat prosaic name, the league at that time was feared and revered on Capitol Hill. Some said it was second in lobbying power only to the National Rifle Association. It funneled huge amounts of money to politicians in every position, then sent its representatives to hoist the flag of home ownership in asking for various breaks. The league controlled virtually every bit of legislation that had anything to do with savings and loans, and it protected the precious deregulation that had given birth to Silverado and hundreds of other institutions like it. Most lawmakers accepted the league's positions. After all, the system seemed to be working, despite the fact that the nation's chief savings and loan regulator was trying desperately to warn of an impending national disaster.

That man was Edwin Gray, who had replaced Dick Pratt in 1983 as chairman of the Federal Home Loan Bank Board. Horrified by early accounts of thrift failures in Texas and increasing reports from his examiners of fraud and wildly speculative thrift dealings across the country, Gray was convinced that the industry was headed for a collapse. He realized that deregulation had inadvertently given savings and loans immense powers that he believed could lead only to ruin. Perhaps it was an oversight, he thought. Perhaps in the flurry of Reagan-era deregulation, Congress simply didn't know what it had done. So Gray quickly assembled a reform package that would close some of the loopholes, tucked it under his arm and began traversing the halls of Congress, knocking on doors to try to win support. But he ran into an obstacle: Mike Wise.

"Everywhere I turned I heard his name," Gray said later. "Wise was the one that was making it all happen. The league had enormous influence, more than any other trade organization of any kind that I can think of. The league at that time wrote all the legislation that came through. No law could be written without the league's approval. Mike wasn't president of the league, but it was assumed that he would be soon. He was very influential. Every year, I sent legislation up to the House and Senate, and each time, it was put on a shelf. Congressmen told me flat out, 'There's nothing that's going to get passed without the league's approval.' I don't think it's stretching it to say that he controlled policy and shaped the direction of the industry."

Wise, who had started in the 1970s in the league's lowest ranks as a member of the subordinate Kansas League of Savings Institutions, so impressed the U.S. League's leaders that they put him on a fast track for its presidency. In 1986, he would be placed on the league's board of directors and its executive committee, which decided who would receive contributions and plotted how the league would achieve its political goals. Wise was a smashing success. "His intellect and his abilities with people were very highly regarded," said Jim Grohl, a league spokesman. Using the winning ways that had enraptured his employees and convinced business leaders of his prowess, Wise won audiences with key senators and congressmen. He argued vehemently for further loosening of regulatory bonds. And most lawmakers were inclined to agree with him. In 1984, Tim Wirth, then a Democratic congressman from Colorado, wrote to Federal Reserve Chairman Paul Volcker recommending Wise for an appointment to the Fed's Consumer Advisory Council. "I can personally attest to his qualifications and his commitment to the public interest," Wirth wrote. "I have had several conversations with him on the subject of financial restructuring in which his thoughtful observations have contributed to my understanding of public policy issues and concerns." Wise was just beginning to flex his political muscle on Capitol Hill. He was soon made president of the Fed's thrift advisory council, and he molded legislation that would infuse money into the ailing Federal Savings and Loan Insurance Fund. By that time, Wise didn't have to go to politicians. They came to him. Wise had become the voice of the savings and loan industry in Washington, and he had a network of contacts that left Gray looking like an eccentric doomsayer. "Boy, was he connected," Gray said. "He was young, intelligent, handsome and he had a way with people. It was tough to fight against that."

A gushing two-page memo written to Wise from Silverado vice chairman Vandapool said it all. "You have presided over this company's transformation from mess to miracle," Vandapool wrote. "You have succeeded in becoming a respected, credible, well- rounded American business leader, industry expert, association chief executive, Colorado advocate and concerned Denverite. You should continue to use that credibility to influence the direction of change—to shape the future of our business—to the benefit of Silverado and all its shareholders."

The entire thrift industry seemed a miracle. The loopholes and concessions opened up by deregulation made overnight success stories of institutions that had struggled only years before. But the truth of the matter was that the industry was in bad shape. Silverado was worse than bad. At the end of 1984, the thrift flirted dangerously with insolvency, having a capital level of only 0.6 percent. And regulators would later find an avalanche of bad loans that Silverado had hidden away or simply not bothered to report. Still, regulators and most people in the thrift business thought Silverado was a model of prosperity, and Wise basked in the golden light of success—the illusion of success. Within a few months, Neil Bush, who was constructing his own illusion of success, would arrive at Silverado's door.

4

The Corruption of Mr. Perfect

It was a small, private affair in the summer of 1985, attended by a few of Denver's new rich. Neil Bush was not yet as wealthy as the other guests, but he had found that he and his wife, Sharon, were welcome among these people as though they were. They enjoyed some notoriety from the fact that Neil's father was vice president. And besides, Neil lived a passably wealthy existence. He would soon draw a six-figure salary from the oil business he had started, despite the fact that it never made money, and he owned a comfortable bungalow close enough to the Country Club neighborhood that the address carried a little weight. He was only 29, after all, and though it wasn't likely he would meet his self-imposed deadline to be independently wealthy by the time he turned 30, that day surely wasn't too far off.

In any case, he liked their new friends. Dinner hadn't yet been served, and the guests stood in small groups, clutching glasses with cocktail napkins. An expensive-looking man excused himself from one of the groups and approached

Neil. "I'm Mike Wise," the man said. "You may know me as chairman of Silverado Banking." The meeting was fortuitous but not coincidental. Wise had set out months before to strengthen Silverado's board of directors, stock it with up-and-comers and well-known names. In a meeting on the subject, a consultant had said, "Why not Neil Bush?" It was a brilliant suggestion, and Wise was immediately taken with it. Arrangements were made to meet. Wise didn't broach the subject of a Silverado directorship at the dinner party. Instead, he chatted with Neil for awhile, letting his charm work. "I liked him right away," Neil said five years later. "I really liked him. I could see that he was well organized and disciplined—all the things I admire and expect in a man. It was clear to me that he was a leader in the industry."

Two weeks after the party, the consultant arranged for a breakfast meeting at a Village Inn pancake house not far from the Country Club neighborhood. Neil ordered an omelette, Wise a fruit plate, and they began to talk. "He told me he wanted me because I was younger than anyone else on the board, that I could add freshness, new blood," Neil recalled. "He said he wanted someone from the oil business, which I was involved in. I never pretended to be an expert in the savings and loan business, and that wasn't what he was looking for." Wise told Neil he didn't want him to make a decision right away. He should think about it, and they would meet again. Neil said he would consider the offer.

A few days later, Wise was on his way to a meeting at Silverado when he stopped a mid-level executive in the hallway. "I'd like to ask your opinion about something," Wise said. "We've been talking to Neil Bush about joining our board. What's your reaction to that?" The point of the question was clear: Wise wasn't interested in business qualifications or background. He was interested in the name. "He didn't need to mention anything," the executive said. "I knew who he was talking about. Neil was starting to be pretty well-known by that time. I got the feeling he was testing out the name-recognition factor. I told him that having the Bush name associated with this institution would be nothing but advantageous." Apparently, it was the response Wise wanted. He smiled and walked away. "I don't think for a minute that he really wanted my advice," the executive said. "I think his mind was already made up, and he was trying to find out how many people recognized the name."

Meanwhile, true to his promise, Neil considered. How could he go wrong? He was flattered and elated by the offer. It fit perfectly in his career plan: Make his fortune in oil, get rooted in the community, increase his influence by making contacts and being associated with the biggest and best businesses in town, then make a move on politics. It was a blueprint laid out neatly by his father, a plan that Neil followed with slavish devotion. He had moved away from home to seek his fortune in Denver, just as Dad had moved away from his family in Greenwich, Connecticut, and Neil had started his own oil company with two friends, just like Dad. Dad's next step had been to join the board of a big Houston bank. Wouldn't a big Denver savings and loan fit the bill for Neil? It seemed the "right thing to do," and, after another breakfast meeting, Neil Bush shook Michael Wise's hand and sealed his fate as poster boy of one of the nation's worst financial crises in history.

Neil Bush's life seemed to be dictated by an intense desire to follow in his father's footsteps. Not only did he appear to use his father's life as a pattern for his own, but Neil also confided from time to time that he was nearly overwhelmed by his father's success, which must have seemed unattainable. "He speaks in awe of his father," said Florian Barth, another Silverado director, late in 1989. "He speaks in awe of the presidency. He speaks in awe of the White House." Indeed, Neil broadcast his feelings to all of Denver during a 1988 news commentary. He had contracted with the local CBS affiliate to air weekly editorials during news broadcasts to discourse about various issues, mostly his father's presidential campaign. One evening he began: "Let me tell you a story about an extraordinary young man . . ." The penetrating news-guy look he had cultivated for the weekly TV spots visibly softened as he listed a roster of accomplishments—winner of the Navy Cross, a Yale graduate who had left home for an unguaranteed life on the barren plains of west Texas. Neil wove a tale of a man who had packed up his clunky red Studebaker and headed West, first to Bakersfield, California, where he took a job selling drill bits for oil wells, then to Midland, Texas, a town sprawled on the flat Texas plains. "You have probably guessed by now, I'm talking about my father," he concluded. "Scholar, war hero, pioneer." Neil uttered the words as though they had echoed in his mind for 100 years. Words to live by. Words to live up to. Neil hadn't even been born when his father moved to Texas, but as he spoke into the camera about the trip, about driving all day and all night, it was as if he saw himself in the back seat, listening to his father's dreams and smelling the hot West Texas wind, which carried promise and the belief that oil wildcatters were the roughest and readiest men in the world. Men like his dad.

Neil came into the world on a wintry Texas day, January 22, 1955, the third son behind Jeb and George Jr., the oldest. By that time, George Sr. had been running his own oil company for five years, and business couldn't have been better. Zapata Exploration (named after the 1952 movie "Viva Zapata," which was playing in downtown Midland when George Sr. and two buddies decided to change the name from Bush Oil Co.) chalked up one success after another. Money flowed in, and the Bush family ascended rapidly, both in wealth and stature. For George Sr., the sense of adventure was thick. He would later write that it was one of the most exciting times of his life.

George tended not to be around the house much. The business took a great deal of his time, and he was already beginning to think about politics. "Mom was the enforcer," Neil told a reporter in 1988. "She was always there. My father was the ultimate authority whenever there was a conflict that couldn't be resolved at the Mom level." In short order, two other children were born—a daughter, Dorothy, and another son, Marvin. The five children quickly dropped into familial molds. George Jr. was the smart one, Doro (Dorothy) the shy one, Marvin the courageous one, Jeb the serious one and Neil the nice one, the good kid. "Of the five, he is the most naive, the most genuine, a classic babe in the woods," a senior White House official told the Washington Post in 1990. For one reason or another, he was the one who did good deeds, stayed out of trouble and generally caused his parents the least grief. When his brothers and sister found reason to be elsewhere, Neil stayed home, mowed the yard and picked up the trash. "He drove us all crazy because he made us look just horrible," said younger brother Marvin.

A family friend said Neil was "Barbara's favorite child. He was her darling. She loves them all, of course, but Neil is very, very dear to her heart." His brothers and sister, too, seemed to cradle Neil as the sweetheart of the family. "He is the most optimistic guy I've ever met in my life," said Marvin in a 1988 interview. "I find that very refreshing." Neil was, in the words of his brothers, "Mr. Perfect."

After George had built a fortune at Zapata, the Bush clan moved from Midland to Houston, where George Sr. expanded his political base, largely by connecting himself with influential Republicans and infiltrating the business community. He won his way onto boards of directors, including that of the First International Bank, a big Houston banking company. Neil watched closely. "I remember thinking that being on a board of directors, especially of a financial institution, is the highest honor there is," he recalled in summer 1990. "I've always had the impression that banks are what build a community. If you're part of a community, that's how you can give back. Not only that, but it improves your standing in the community. It's an important service, one that should be respected."

For George Sr., the strategy worked. In 1966, he was elected to Congress, and the family packed off to Washington. Young Neil, eleven years old at the time, was terribly impressed. Shortly after the election, he reportedly beamed to a stranger sitting next to him on an airplane: "My father's going to be president." Neil enjoyed the celebrity of it as well. His father was an important man, and by association, Neil felt he was important. And so the move to Washington, where important people are a dime a dozen, was a shock. "There I was with a heavy Texas accent, white socks and a crew cut," Neil told a reporter in 1988. "I had a terrible first half-year. I got zapped into D.C. before I could enjoy any celebrity in Houston. I was just another kid on the block."

Washington proved a difficult time for Neil. Not only was he just another kid on the block, it began to be clear that he wasn't quite as smart as the other Bush children. Sure, he was a good kid, but accomplishments didn't seem to come as easily to Neil as they did for his siblings. This realization came shortly after arriving in Washington, when Neil enrolled in St. Albans, a private prep school. Neil was the first in his family not to follow his father to Phillips Academy in Andover, Massachusetts. St. Albans is prestigious enough in its own right, but it wasn't Dad's school.

St. Albans is the vision of prepster academia. Perched on the highest hill in Washington, its gothic, ivy-covered walls gaze pacifically across the city while Episcopalian masters thrust letters upon their boys. Over the years, it has counted on its rolls the sons of Kennedys, Gore, Jackson, Buckley, Mondale. Indeed, so many political-types attend that the masters, quick to discipline those who try to gain favor from their names, use the phrase: "Your father may be making history, but you still have to pass it." Neil arrived a stubble-headed eleven-year-old, naive and out of place. Academic life was "the biggest shock for me as a boy," Neil said twenty-two years later. He couldn't seem to do anything right. He brought home poor marks, and no one knew why. But he kept at it. His English teacher sent his papers back marked "with what seemed like hundreds of misspellings and grammatical corrections," and he was forced to come in on weekends to write those words over and over again. Things didn't get much better, and finally, a school counselor told Neil's mother that it didn't look as if the boy was going to make it. The counselor was sorry, but it was doubtful Neil had the potential to graduate. Barbara said the hell with doubtful potential, and with the matronly fire she's become known for as First Lady, she set about helping her son.

Neil's problem was dyslexia, a fairly common disorder that impairs the brain's ability to interpret printed symbols. A dyslexic is prone to transpose letters and words, and words can sometimes seem to be out of order in a sentence. If the impairment isn't spotted, dyslectics generally have a difficult time learning to read, and they fall behind in almost all subject areas, descending into confusion as their peers advance. Most teachers now are trained to look for the signs of dyslexia, and it's not considered a career-stopping problem. But at the time, not as much was known about the disorder, and it was lumped with other learning disabilities into a broad set of mental deficiencies. But Barbara was determined not to let this demon take her son. She spent hours with him, pushing him through exercises consisting mainly of reading practice. The exercises are more painful than they sound. They require monk-like discipline, concentrating on letters and words so that they aren't transposed in the mind. Neil said his mother spent endless hours with him, and he spent hours more alone in his room and in remedial classes. Finally, his grades improved, and Neil managed to get along well enough. "He didn't stand out for good or for bad," a former teacher recalled. "He did what he had to do. He did his job."

As time went on, he became more comfortable with the new life he led. He became the sort of guy everyone liked. "So many of these kids were political products," said John Davis, St. Albans headmaster, who also taught a required religion course. "They were very careful about how and when to use their names—they were brought up that way, dealt with life that way. But Neil seemed oblivious to that. He was very much like his mother, very open, warm, never on his guard. I think he assumed that people are all basically decent." When Neil graduated from St. Albans in 1973, he quoted an unknown author in his yearbook: "A man's true wealth is the good he does in the world."

With that nugget of wisdom, he left Washington for college. Dad had gone to Yale. So had George Jr. Indeed, over a third of St. Albans graduates end up in the Ivy League. But prep school counselors warned him of following in those footsteps. "I'm always careful to tell my boys not to be too eager to follow father or brother. If they don't get in or they get in and fail, there's too much room for inferiority feelings. It's not worth it." So Neil applied to Rice University in Houston and Tulane in New Orleans. "I think he wanted to get away from the East Coast," the counselor said. "He wanted to be in the somewhat freer environment of the West."

Rice eventually dropped out of the picture, so Tulane it was. For the first time—even though he wasn't at Dad's school—Neil began to feel as though he could be a scholar, too. He tackled his courses with a vigor he had never shown at St. Albans, and he proved to be a worthy student. "He was bright, he was articulate, his exams were well-written. He was eager to learn, and it showed," said Jean Danielson, a political science professor who taught Western political thought. Among his classmates (who happened to include the son of CIA director William Casey), Neil became a fixture of sorts, even a leader. He joined the school's political science honorary society, Pi Sigma Delta, and he emerged as someone people remembered and respected. More than a decade after Neil graduated, a Latin American exchange student reminded a professor that he was in Neil Bush's class. "I was new to the school, I was new to the United States," the student told his professor. "Neil came to me and took care of me. He went out of his way to help, did everything he could for me. I'll always be grateful for that."

More than ever, Neil drew inspiration from his father. George, who was advancing through the ranks of government, became ambassador to China while Neil was at Tulane, and one summer Neil went to visit. "He came in to show me pictures, just snapshots of the trip," Professor Danielson said.

"He was so excited. You could see, really feel, the warmth that he felt for his parents, especially his father. Complete admiration. At one point, I remember Neil's dad came to speak to the class. Neil was so excited to see him—you could tell that there was no one in the world he would have rather seen."

Neil finished his degree in 1977 with a 3.2 grade point average and went to work for a year on George Jr.'s narrowly unsuccessful campaign for the 18th congressional district in Texas. Neil struggled in the shadow of his older sibling. "Neil was, I don't know, just a nerd," a campaign worker said. "I don't know how to put it. He tried to win people, but he tried too hard. He was like a little kid, always pulling stunts like blowing up balloons and letting the air out, you know, to make a certain sound. George had a lot of friends who were country-club types, and they gave him a lot of rope. But it was like they put up with him because he was George's brother.

"To see them together was like night and day. George was mature and grown up, self-confident and in control of himself. Neil was the eternal kid brother."

Still, the experience fired Neil's imagination. He had entertained fantasies about his own career in politics, but he never spoke about them. When he returned to Tulane to complete a master's degree in business administration, it was all he could talk about—the rush of the campaign, selling ideas, selling a candidate. This was the real world. This was the stuff that made history. And so, when he joined his father's 1980 presidential campaign, he knew he'd found his calling. It was an exhilarating time that changed his life, he said later. He was in charge of a small portion of the campaign, raising money and managing a few dozen of his father's followers. He stood shoulder-to-shoulder with his father in the battle pit of politics, and he loved every minute of it. Not only did he love the politics, but he loved being near his father. He said at the time that he had never seen more of him than during that campaign. Indeed, it was a childhood dream. As long as he could remember, he had wanted to help his father become president. And he nurtured the idea that someday, after cutting his teeth on a few George Bush campaigns, he would be the candidate.

Politics had to wait, however. Fate had it that love would come first. While knocking on doors for his father before the New Hampshire primary, a Republican impatiently interrupted his campaign pitch to inquire, "Are you married?" He wasn't, and so he was led by the arm and introduced to a school teacher named Sharon. Bright, with a sort of sorority-girl lightness about her, Sharon won his heart in short order, and they were married months later.

Long before, Neil had begun to plot the course of his career. If he couldn't go to his father's schools, he could follow his father's steps into the business that had made him rich and catapulted him into politics. "I didn't have a red Studebaker," Neil said in 1988. "But I wanted to be in the oil business." Whereas oil had meant Texas a few years before, in 1979, oil meant Denver. He had heard the stories of the wealth being made there. But Denver represented more than wealth. By going there, he could do exactly as his father had done: split with his family. "That's why I came here," he said in 1990, "to do something different, assert my independence." So he secured an interview with Amoco Production Co., packed up his car and went West.

The meeting at Amoco went well, as far as it goes. The company offered him a job as a trainee to become a landman, which is oil industry parlance for someone who secures leases for mineral rights on other people's property. Typically, oil companies buy, sell and trade leases in such a way that the leases become a sort of currency, and big oil companies employ hundreds of landmen. It's mostly paper-shuffling, and at $30,000 a year, Neil thought he deserved more. So he and Sharon piled back into the car and headed for Wyoming to check out some other contacts Neil had made. At the time, Wyoming was booming with oil exploration. Its economy was fat, and it was one of a number of Western states with otherwise dreary reputations that were cashing in on oil reserves. Millionaires were being made. But dreary reputations are created for a reason. The long highway north into Wyoming snakes through hundreds of miles of empty plains, through towns named Chugwater and Wheatland. It's an empty place, and even the economic boom had succeeded only in producing a proliferation of trailer homes for wildcatters, reputed to be mean, hard-living souls. It wasn't long before Sharon began to look sick. "I don't think she, with her New England background, was very happy about what she saw out there," a friend said. So they turned the car around and went back to Denver. Neil took the Amoco job and they settled down. It couldn't be worse than selling drill bits in Bakersfield, California.

They moved into an apartment and set about the business of having a family and climbing the social ladder. It didn't take long. Even without money, the Bush name sat well with people, and soon they were invited to the correct parties and the right functions. Neil "didn't have a business reputation, he had a name," said Marvin Buckles, executive vice president of Denver's Bank Western Federal Savings. "He was the darling of the young, yuppie social set, the local charity ball set. He and his wife both photographed well at cocktails." Neil became a board member of charitable organizations like the Boys Club and Children's Museum. He also joined the board of the Denver Club, an exclusive establishment where business-types power-lunched. (The club had a "squash component, too," Neil pointed out to government lawyers investigating him in 1990. "Not squash the food, squash the sport.")

Sharon, meanwhile, did her own climbing. Among the monied set, social climbing means charity. The most fashionable charities attract the richest and most important people. This was where Sharon put her efforts. At first, she didn't have much success getting in with the best and the latest. But she scored a coup of sorts by teaming late in 1982 with Nancy Davis Zarif, daughter of Marvin Davis, the oil billionaire. Sharon and Nancy formed Cookie Express, which delivered giant cookies to people's homes. It wasn't a charity, but Nancy Davis Zarif was the correct company. It earned Sharon her debut into Denver's social columns, and her stock increased. "That cookie thing was the most ridiculous little scheme I've ever seen," said a Denver society matron, who later came to know Sharon. "Everybody thought so, and it only lasted a couple months. But I'll tell you something: Nancy Davis got the Bushes onto invitation lists. I don't think it was Neil who got them into parties. I think it was Sharon." She worked her way up through a series of lesser balls and galas until she finally landed the chairmanship of the Children's Hospital Gala, second in stature only to Marvin Davis' Carousel Ball. Later, she founded Karitas Foundation, which sells toys and children's clothing across the country to raise money for children's charities.

Between parties, the Bushes found time for three children—Lauren, Ashley and Pierce—who were honored by the Denver media with a certain amount of celebrity as they came into the world. It was a happy time, more or less, and Neil reveled in the attention. He was quickly gaining notoriety around town. People liked him, and businessmen seemed to want to know him. At business luncheons and charity galas he hopped from table to table, shaking hands and introducing himself. "Neil doesn't come across as someone who would sit at the table and arm wrestle with you," said Marvin Wolf, a Denver oilman. "He's just a nice guy." Florian Barth, the Silverado director, said: "He plays everything down. Unless you really chased him down about it, you wouldn't even know he was the vice president's son. He didn't drive a fancy car. I used to rib him all the time. I'd ask him: 'Why the hell aren't you driving a Lincoln, a man of your position?' He'd just laugh. Neil was an old shoe. He was about as straight an arrow as there is."

Former Colorado Attorney General Duane Woodard tells a story about a ritzy black-tie affair he attended. Neil and Sharon and most of Denver's dignitaries and important business people were there. As the evening closed, Neil shook hands with people around him, smiling and joking, obviously enjoying the status his name brought him. But as the guests filed out, Neil dug in his pockets and, chagrined, found nothing. "Hey Duane," he said. "Could I borrow a couple bucks from you for parking? I don't seem to have any cash."

It wasn't long before he would begin uttering a variation of those words to raise money to start his oil business. That had been his dream all along, to start a junior version of Zapata. He had talked of it from the time he settled in Denver. With the dream tucked away, he worked hard in Amoco's training program, traveling every once in a while from the black-glass Amoco tower in downtown Denver to an oil field in northeastern Colorado called the Denver Julesburg Basin. There, he got his boots dirty and learned the business of buying and selling leases. Soon, he was cutting his own deals, and he liked the work. There was a problem, however. Denver was blazing with oil money. Amoco and a lot of other people were getting rich, stinking rich. Not Neil. He was making 30 grand doing the work for somebody else.

He took to talking with coworkers about his plan for an oil business. One of them, a geologist named James Judd, shared his ambition. Oil prices were climbing all the time, and the people who got it out of the ground could make some money. Together, they approached Evans Nash, a geophysicist who had left Amoco a year earlier to do consulting work. Nash had a beautiful plan. In the northeastern reaches of Wyoming was a place oilmen knew as the Powder River Basin. A particular variety and age of geological formation was found there, he explained, and where they found that formation, they would surely find oil. Lots of it. The plan seemed bulletproof. "I thought we were going to clean up unbelievably," Nash said later.

So they organized a partnership, calling it JNB Exploration, using the first letter of each of their last names. The exploration expert would be Nash, since he had the background. Judd took the responsibility of dealing with leases. Neil was in charge of finances and a variety of other jobs like retaining attorneys, receiving and disbursing funds, writing quarterly reports and keeping records. But his chief duty was to open doors and bring in money. He didn't have much in the way of technical expertise, but he had something else: a name. "Neil knew people because of his name," Nash said in 1990. "He's the one who got us going. He's the one that made it happen for us." Neil was unabashed in his role. He "served as kind of an expediter," Neil explained to government investigators who inquired in 1990 about the rivers of money that cascaded from wealthy investors into JNB. "I mean, it was my job within JNB to, just to expedite those sorts of things."

Neil insisted it wasn't his name that opened people's wallets. Indeed, he claimed to take steps to avoid such things with his "Smith Smell Test," designed to detect whether Neil Smith would get the same treatment as Neil Bush. If Neil Bush got a better deal under the test, "I would automatically reject it," he declared. But his actions didn't support his words. While out looking for JNB investors, he left a message with a wealthy Denver oilman's secretary. "Tell him Neil Bush called," he reportedly said. "You know, the vice president's son." Later, in a 1989 interview, he said: "I can't deny that my name helped me to meet people. Maybe they were attracted to that. I don't know." Mr. Perfect had become The Expediter.

5

Men of Means

In late 1982, The Expediter placed a call to Bill L. Walters Cos. The call was the first of his money-seeking missions. JNB needed cash to get started, and while Neil was beginning to live his life among the rich and famous, his name had so far earned him only half that description. Neither he nor his partners at JNB possessed the means to throw cash into an unproven enterprise, even if it was their own. Until they struck it rich—it wouldn't be long, in their estimation—they needed people to pay their salaries, provide working capital and shoulder most of the risk.

Neil had racked his brain for possible sources and hit at last on his new friend, the wealthy and powerful Bill Walters. The two weren't really friends, not in the way that most people would define such a relationship. Rather, they had met some months before at one of the power lunches Neil had taken to attending. They had shaken hands, and Neil had introduced himself. *You know, the vice president's son.* Walters had seemed to take an instant liking to the young man.

Walters' secretary sent the call through. Neil reminded Walters of their lunch meeting and explained his plan. The company would need a $150,000 investment from Walters in exchange for a 6.25 percent share in the profits. Neil would put in $100 of his own money for a 32 percent share. He quickly explained that the JNB plan virtually guaranteed that Walters could expect—if their calculations were correct—a quick return on his money. Neil finished his pitch, and Walters agreed to meet with Neil and his partners.

A week later, Neil and his two partners sat in the richly appointed lobby of Walters' office. The man from whom they were about to beg money sat squarely on top of the pyramid of Denver's rich and influential. Walters was a real estate developer, and the sifting bin of human hierarchy in the late 1970s and early '80s had shaken real estate developers to the top of the pile. It was true in other parts of the country (witness Donald Trump), and it certainly was true in Denver. Civic and business leaders looked upon real estate developers as prophets of prosperity because they possessed what people in the business call vision. They spoke of great glittering dreams—office parks, shopping malls, condos— that would allow Denver to shake off its spit- in-the-dust reputation and become a real city.

What's more, the oil boom had sparked growth like no one had ever seen in Denver. The developers who built places for all these new people to work, live and spend their money were becoming unfathomably rich. They handed out cash donations to the symphony, the art museum, hospitals, libraries and so on. With people like that around, Denver wasn't going to be a second- rate cow town for long, and they were afforded regal status.

Of Denver's real estate lords, Walters was the king. People called him "Golden Boy" and "the Donald Trump of Denver." (It was a compliment at the time.) By the mid '80s, a competitor conceded that "the son of a bitch controls the market." From his office in Southeast Denver, Walters could survey a kingdom of office buildings and condominiums that in less than a decade had helped make him a millionaire two hundred times over. At his peak, he controlled more building space and raw land than exists in all of downtown Denver, owned four banks and enough companies and

partnerships to fill two file drawers of microfiched government records. In 1987, Denver's business community made
him chairman of the Greater Denver Chamber of Commerce.
He ferried himself about the city in a Mercedes or a convert-
ible Rolls Royce or a Bentley, depending on the day, and
retired evenings to his mansion in the privately patrolled
Polo Club neighborhood. "Let me put it to you this way," a
friend said. "If you could have looked in the dictionary under
Big Cheese, you would have found Bill's picture."

Walters' rise to big-cheese status originated from begin-
nings as humble as those of the next developer. With a degree
in architecture from the University of Kansas, where he
played football with the legendary Gale Sayers, Walters
moved to Denver in 1972. He set up a drafting table in his
basement and declared he'd soon be the richest man in town.
He didn't have money to speak of, but what difference did
that make? As any number of late-night TV seminars will tell
you, the secret to making a lot of money in the real estate
business is not to use your own cash. Never, never put
yourself at risk. That was a cardinal rule whose corollary was:
Wealth can be created from nothing. And that's what Walters
did. He talked an insurance company into putting up the
money for a condominium project in a mountain resort town.
"I optioned the ground, designed the building, had 'em built
and had 'em sold. That was sort of the beginning of a track
record I built for being able to borrow money."

That was the key—convincing people to give him
money— and Walters was extraordinary at it. Perpetually
suntanned, with waves of athletic hair and an enormous gold
Rolex on his arm, he had "this ability to ingratiate himself
with the right people—lenders, top-flight brokers," said Jack
Box, a Denver real estate broker who worked for Walters. In
the late '70s, after a few more condo projects, each one a little
bigger and better than the last, Walters took that charm to
National Mortgage, a Denver financing company. He'd had
enough of rinky-dink deals and wanted to play with the big
boys. He had a strip mall in mind. He would design it, build
it and, God willing, sell it for a small fortune. Everyone

would be rich if he could just get a loan. National Mortgage agreed. "Bill was just another face in the crowd at the time, just another developer getting started," said the loan officer who cut the deal. "He was a younger guy doing business on his savvy, and he had a lot of that. So we lent him the money."

Less than a year later, Denver was graced with a new strip mall, and Walters was graced with a small fortune. "It was his first really big deal, and I'll tell you something: That boy made a ton of dough off that one," the National Mortgage loan officer said. The deal went so well, in fact, that Walters wanted to do more, so he took the loan officer for a ride in his new Mercedes. They purred along the silky black asphalt of freshly laid roads snaking like rivers through Walters' latest project. The developer shouted to be heard over the wind as he waved a palm toward a half-dozen construction cranes extracting steel skeletons from the rolling Colorado plains. "These are just the start," he was saying. "We want a whole office complex, with shopping, restaurants and possibly supporting residential areas over there." He pointed through the windshield, beyond the sound of arc welders and cement trucks, to empty grassland. "I firmly believe this is very promising, and I'd like to have you in with me if you're interested." The loan officer was overwhelmed. "Bill was just too goddamned big for us. It was too much. There wasn't a local lender who could get him the kind of money he needed."

Fortunately for Walters, it turned out that for the time being, he didn't need local lenders or lenders at all, for that matter. In 1981, the government handed him a blank check in the form of a tax break. Congress had decided that the country's sagging economy needed a pick-me-up. Interest rates had soared so high that Congress believed it wasn't worth anybody's while to borrow money to construct office buildings and shopping centers. So, under the approving eye of the Reagan administration, lawmakers passed the Economic Recovery Tax Act, another way of saying Big Tax Break. In theory, the act simply made a tax shelter out of commercial real estate to encourage ordinary Americans to

give their dollars to developers. The developers would construct buildings, creating jobs for construction workers, who
would spend money on clothes and refrigerators, creating
jobs for haberdashers and appliance salesmen and so on
down the line. At the time, it made perfect sense. But in fact,
it ripped a gaping hole in the fabric of checks and balances
that kept commercial construction in step with the nation's
growth.

Before the tax act, real estate investors (most of whom
made their daily bread by carefully watching the market and
looking for good opportunities) would sink money into a
prospective project only if it looked as if rent-paying tenants
would move in once it was completed. An investor only
made money on a shopping center if shoe stores and food
courts and boutiques were willing to pay rent for the
privilege of doing business there. But the act made the tax
breaks so good that it didn't matter anymore whether
anybody needed or even wanted the project. An investor
could buy a share of a real estate project for $100,000 and get
$200,000 in tax breaks. Suddenly, well-to-do doctors and
lawyers and stock brokers—anybody who had a few bucks
to protect from Uncle Sam, people who never before had
dreamed of investing in commercial real estate—handed
over their wallets to people like Walters.

The fatal flaw in the act was that it assumed real estate
developers would use investors' money in the best interests
of their communities, which is a little like giving your Master-
Card to a kid in a candy store and assuming he'll buy what's
good for him. Real estate developers seem to be driven by a
hormone that requires them to do a deal whenever they've
got money enough to do it. They are restrained from building
only by investors who cut off the cash when things start
looking bad. So Walters and developers like him built to their
hearts' content, cranking out office parks and shopping
centers with other people's money and making fortunes
selling the projects once they were done. Nobody could lose
because property values went through the roof as

speculators nearly went hysterical bidding for prairie acreage- cum-office parks.

By 1982, Walters was the king of Denver's real estate establishment. He bought the mansion, the cars, the Rolex and a pair of massive gold cufflinks with his initials carved on them. "They were sort of a symbol that he had made it," a friend said. He traveled with an entourage of lawyers, who grouped around him like court advisers, directed by nods and raised fingers. At city council meetings of a Denver suburb, for example, Walters requested rezoning and modifications on covenants at virtually every meeting. The man with the suntan and the Rolex stood before the lectern and announced his intentions, then sat placidly in the shadows while his court advisers bullied and argued and sweated before the council. In rare interviews with the press, Walters sat in his office chair as if it were a throne, and the lawyers fairly kneeled at his side, intercepting questions and offering up answers.

Still, he liked to come off as a regular guy. He spoke softly and carried a lot of money, and people loved him. He regularly lunched at a little restaurant near his office. It's a dark place fashioned after a medieval British ale house. Painted Styrofoam simulates big wooden beams on the ceiling, and Coors Light is served in fake pewter tankards. When he paraded in one blazing summer day, an elderly waitress cooed with delight as he draped an affectionate arm around her while a younger waitress asked shyly if she could take his coat. Walters flashed his straight, white teeth and made motions as though they might kiss his hand. "Isn't he wonderful?" the elderly waitress exclaimed to the younger one, after proudly leading Walters by the elbow to his table.

Other developers were doing deals and doing very nicely, but Walters did them bigger and better than anyone else. To do that, he needed people on his side. And sometimes getting people on your side requires more than good looks and charm. He set up a political action committee—funded by $5,000 and $10,000 donations from people who worked for him, including his secretary—and it funneled hundreds of thousands of dollars into the campaigns of city councilmen, county commissioners and mayors.

Walters also apparently used other methods to keep people on his side. One of them was God. Former employees said Walters brought his people together each morning to solemnly pray. *Lord, show me the way to non-recourse financing and full occupancy at $48 a square foot.*

It was beginning to snow outside. Neil fidgeted in the chair. It had been fifteen minutes since he and his partners had given Walters' secretary their names. Finally, the suntan strolled from his office, flashing straight, white teeth and extending a big fleshy palm. The court advisers appeared, and the entourage whisked into a conference room. For a half hour, Walters sat silently, leaning back in his chair, fingertips together, as Judd and Nash shuffled documents, proposals, maps and diagrams. The court advisers scribbled notes. Neil sat with hands folded. They finished, and Walters leaned forward. "With all this you've given me, I ought to go out and do it myself and not even fool with you guys." A flash from the teeth. "Thanks for coming by." After they left, Walters instructed his lawyers to draft an agreement.

With $150,000 from Walters and another $150,000 from an independent oil company, JNB officially opened for business on January 6, 1983. Neil quit Amoco and set up shop in his new office, a bust of his father on the credenza behind him and his grandfather's nameplate on the desk before him. Now, he was a Bush. Now, he was like Dad. And, thanks to Walters, he was making $66,000, a nice little raise from $30,000 at Amoco.

Still, $300,000 wasn't going to keep them alive for long. Salaries and office overhead alone would eat away that capital without any left over for exploration and drilling. The Expediter had work to do. It happened that Walters had a friend in the real estate business named Ken Good. Good was second in stature only to Walters, though for opulence he would soon surpass the king. They were kindred spirits in the sense that they made their money in more or less the same fashion and that they had more of it than either of them knew what to do with. Money had ceased to be anything but a symbol of their greatness, and they wielded it with a bravado that had made them famous in Denver. Nearly every weekend they chartered a jet and flew to Las Vegas, Atlantic City or Monte Carlo to drop hundreds of thousands of dollars. "In Vegas, the Strip wouldn't take bets big enough, so they always went downtown to the Golden Nugget and played blackjack at $50,000 a hand," said a friend who accompanied them. "$100,000 didn't mean anything to these guys. They'd lose five, six, seven hundred thousand a night and it was all in a day's work. They were both crap shooters."

On one of these trips, Walters and Good were in the midst of a real estate deal. Walters was buying property from Good, and negotiations had reached an impasse $100,000 apart. "They settled the difference in a Las Vegas casino when Good suggested they just cut a deck of cards for the money," another friend said. "That's the way they played, and that's the way they ran their businesses."

And so it was a bit of fortune when, in summer 1983, Neil received an elaborately engraved invitation to visit the new estate of Ken Good. Good didn't have Walters' country-club good looks, but in his own way he cut a distinctive figure. He was bald on top with a wreath of black hair that descended along his cheeks into a massive coffee-colored beard whose length regularly changed. Good explained once that he trimmed his beard in accordance with his prosperity: When he felt rich and deals were going down, it grew long, and when the cards didn't fall to his liking, he cut it close. Likewise, in good times he wore a peevish grin and his eyes glimmered so that he looked for all the world like an elf working in Keebler's magic kitchen. But when things didn't go right, his brow corrugated and his eyebrows arched in a terrifying, satanic glower.

The party was to celebrate the opening of Good's new $10 million house, the largest home in Colorado. It had fifteen bathrooms (all decorated with exotic marbles and woods), six kitchens (one of them a catering kitchen with mirror-finished Italian cabinets and stainless steel-edged granite counter tops), a wine cellar, guest suites and private offices in case visitors wanted to work during their stay.

Liquor was pumped throughout the house via special plumbing from drums of scotch, gin and vodka in the wine cellar. In the master bathroom, a huge plate glass wall allowed "you to sit on the crapper and get one of the best views in the city," said one real estate agent. The mansion was saturated with electronic toys and hidden rooms. One of them appeared to be a bomb shelter, sealed by two secret stainless steel doors, encased in concrete and containing a telephone with a direct line to the Denver Police Department.

The house was equipped with its own health club, which included an indoor frontennis court (frontennis is a close cousin of jai alai), a racquetball court, bicycle trainers, an electric massage table, a 150-gallon saline flotation tub and marble- walled men's and women's locker rooms. The women's locker room had a unique feature, according to a bit of Good mansion mythology. Some who attended Good's numerous bashes insisted that a wall-length mirror inside was in reality a one-way mirror that allowed guests outside at the pool to view the disrobing within.

All 33,000 square feet of Good's house sprawled on five acres of hilltop south of the city, where he could gaze toward the Rocky Mountains through huge glass walls, unimpeded by other buildings. "It was a goddamn country club," a developer of more modest means recalled.

The mansion was decorated with enormous works of art, which Good said was his obsession. He declared himself an amateur collector, but when one has money, why settle for the usual knickknacks? He purchased a massive kinetic sculpture by Yaacov Agam of Israel that was controlled by a computerized panel so complex that Good admitted he didn't know how to operate it. The artist was a guest of honor at one of Good's parties, where he delighted other guests by drawing grease-pencil caricatures on the $200-a-plate china and handing them to whoever wanted one.

The estate was littered with other enormous works, including pieces by Christo, known for wrapping islands in Miami's Biscayne Bay in pink cellophane. Among his furniture was a dining table said to have belonged to Henry VIII.

Ken Good loved his money, and he loved showing it off. The louder, the bigger, the better. By 1984, he roared around town in his maroon Maserati. If he loved one thing more than money, it was parties. He threw them often and attended other people's even more often. He arrived at the annual Ascot Picnic, sponsored by the Rolls-Royce owners club, wearing a white dinner jacket, top hat, cane and tennis shorts. It was the sort of statement that endeared him to people.

Good, like Walters, had built his empire on the no-money-down method of real estate development. After making and losing a small fortune in Dallas, Good came to Denver in 1979. His first project was a condo development in Denver's Capitol Hill area, a fashionable but mixed inner-city neighborhood. From there, he bought and sold raw land and eventually put together a deal for the largest residential development in the state. He took risks that would have terrified more faint-hearted developers, and his financial existence hung perpetually on the precipice of disaster. A compatriot said Good lived on the impulse to "buy, buy, buy, bigger, bigger, bigger." He got financing for his deals in manic dashes from one banker to the next and gut-wrenching all-night negotiating sessions, on which he thrived. "Ken Good is a riverboat gambler," said an executive of his Florida-based Gulfstream Corp., which he purchased shortly before leaving Denver in the late 1980s, "not a businessman."

"He was a compulsive gambler in the true, pathological sense of the word," said the friend who accompanied him to Las Vegas. "He would be the first to admit that. He had to have the risk. He had to be out on the edge."

His compulsiveness, some friends believe, sprang from an impoverished childhood as the son of an itinerant Methodist minister in LaCrosse, Kansas. "To spend a dollar at a restaurant once in a year was a big treat," a close friend said. "I think he spent the better part of his childhood dreaming about spending incredible amounts of money. And when he finally did it, he did it in spades."

What Good lacked in wealth during his high school years, he made up for in self-promotion. At LaCrosse High School, where he was a basketball player, prom court member and regional debate champion, a classmate recalls: "He was the kind of guy that if you could buy him for what he was worth and sell him for what he thought he was worth, you'd make money."

His real estate career was inspired by one of his college lecturers at Southern Methodist University, millionaire Texas developer Trammell Crow. Three years after graduating from SMU in 1966, the young developer set up Good Financial Corp. and bought $250 million in Texas real estate in a few short years of frenzied buying. Then disaster struck the Texas real estate market, and his budding empire collapsed. So he moved to Denver.

There, in the tradition of big-time developers of the age, Good conjured up a significant portion of his money in elaborate deals that created wealth where none had been— with a little help from obliging savings and loans like Silverado. For example, Good and several partners traded two parcels of vacant land three times in six months with the value increasing each time until they finally sold them to Silverado for a $3.2 million profit. Good and Walters had become two of Silverado's most reliable customers. Each had taken out millions in Silverado loans, and they had helped Silverado recapitalize itself in 1984. Silverado was desperately short of capital, so it had come up with a scheme to raise it by issuing stock in exchange for real estate. In the deal, Silverado traded shares of its stock for raw land from both developers, issuing $15 million in stock to Walters and $14 million to Good. The thrift then included the land in its capital. Walters and Good were given royal treatment at Silverado, where they were allowed to use Wise's private elevator to the Skydeck. A Silverado executive recalled: "Ken Good had a reputation —well, it wasn't the best. But I figured if Mike was keeping company with him, he must be okay."

Neil probably didn't know or particularly care about the sources of Good's wealth when he and Sharon, in tuxedo and ball gown, urged their Volvo along the cobbled circle drive that swept past the great stainless steel doors of Good's mansion. They waited in a long line of black limousines as each paused to spill its guests, who offered gloved hands to valets. Sequins and jewelry glimmered in great fountains of light placed among the trees, and the sound of pampered laughter tinkled luxuriantly across the lawn. "All the great and near-great of the city were there," said a friend who attended. "Mayors, senators, the governor, business people, friends . . . everybody who was anybody. Ken just sat down and invited anyone he ever knew and quite a few people that he didn't."

Neil and Sharon made their way along a massive white hallway, hung with oil paintings as though it were a museum. The hallway opened at last onto a balcony looking over the expansive frontennis court, transformed for the occasion into a virtual garden where guests ate and danced and drank. The buffet table, surrounded by swans carved in ice, held poached salmon and steamed lobster.

Presently, Bill Walters approached Neil and introduced the party's host. Things must have been going well for Good; his brow was smooth and his beard was long.

Good must have been delighted to meet Neil. He made it a point to foster relationships within circles of power and on their peripheries, and he had a long track record of exploiting those relationships. In the early 1980s, for example, Good had struck up a friendship with Jack Kinstlinger, head of Colorado's Department of Highways. The two lunched occasionally, and before long Good heaped upon him the graciousness of his lifestyle. Good made him a regular guest at wild parties at his Vail vacation house and hosted him at a charity ball. A little more than a year after they became friends, Kinstlinger oversaw a state purchase of Good land for a stretch of highway that allegedly paid the developer $2 million more than the land was worth.

That relationship wasn't the first Good apparently nurtured for his own gain. In 1980, Good began dating the executive director of Colorado's Department of Local Affairs, Paula Herzmark. He showered her with gifts—thousands of dollars in jewelry, clothes and precious art. "You start buying mink coats, things like that, it mounts in a hurry," Good said at the time. "I know from experience." After they had known each other a while, Good launched what turned out to be an unsuccessful takeover bid for a huge oil shale operation, Tosco Corp., in western Colorado. During a vitriolic nine-month battle that turned into a financial fencing match, Tosco executives charged that Good appeared to have access to secret government information about their company. They filed suit, alleging that Herzmark was leaking the information to her lover. During the ensuing state ethics investigation, which eventually found no wrongdoing, Good received a note in the mail. "Don't let the bastards get you down," it read. "You're a good guy doing good things." It was signed by then Colorado Governor Dick Lamm, who was a regular on Good's invitation list.

Those relationships appeared to be part of Good's strategy, which he wrote down in a memo to his associates on January 21, 1981. Among other things, he wrote that he wanted to do the biggest land and development deals in the state, and in announcing them to the public, he wanted to hold grand receptions and dinners for the most prominent government officials and influential community leaders. Good reasoned that because he was planning the "largest land deal in Colorado history" and a "billion-dollar" development, he would "merit tremendous media coverage" and "front-page news." He intended to make friends with anyone possessing an ounce of power to make himself one of Denver's "key policy-makers," he wrote, and he set a goal to "become better acquainted with the movers and shakers throughout the state of Colorado (to) expand my political power base and influence."

Whether or not Good was attempting to expand his political base with Neil Bush, he took the young man under his wing. Neil told him of his plans to make it big, and Good told Neil he wanted to expand his holdings into oil exploration. It seemed as though they could help each other out. Weeks later, Good made arrangements to acquire 25 percent of JNB and put $10,000 into the partnership. The money itself was almost meaningless. Ten thousand dollars wouldn't have lasted a week if the company was serious about drilling. "It was nothing more than a way to make a valid contract," said Neil's partner, Evans Nash. "It was just so he could get ownership in the company and start getting us the capital we needed." With his ownership interest in place, Good went to Cherry Creek National Bank, one of the banks that Walters owned, and acquired two lines of credit for JNB worth a total of $1.5 million.

It was 1984. JNB had struck oil a couple of times, but after ecstatic celebrations, the wells proved to be too small to make any money, and they were abandoned. It was maddening, considering how well the plan worked on paper, but it wasn't altogether unexpected. Industry literature at the time suggested that only one hole in twelve would produce enough oil to be profitable. In any case, JNB provided a nice existence for Neil. Or, rather, Ken Good did. Good allowed—in fact, he entreated—Neil to use his magnificent estate. He wanted Neil and his partners to come out each morning and join him in daily workouts at his health club. Good was manic about exercise. Athletics strengthen the mind and expunge demons from the soul, he said, demons like doubt and indecision. He didn't like those things in himself, and he didn't like to see them in others. "He got us all involved," Nash said. "He liked to see us out there working out, enjoying his place." Neil took to running laps around the grounds in good weather, breathing the pine-scented air and listening to horses neigh in nearby pastures. The rolling hills of the estate and soft light that played through the trees were therapeutic and invigorating. On occasion, he played racquetball on the indoor court or lifted weights. A masseuse was available after the workout.

JNB meetings were held at the estate. The partners gathered every couple of weeks to go over JNB's progress in a palatial conference room that streamed with sunlight and hummed with electronic gadgetry. Good usually arrived in workout clothes, sometimes still carrying his tennis racket. "He just sat there and listened," Nash recalled. "He was a very friendly man. But sometimes you can get this feeling about someone. I felt like he was our best friend as long as things went his way. It was like things were too good to be true, and if things didn't work out the way he wanted, he could get pretty nasty. It was just a feeling."

But Good was good to Neil. In 1984, he told Neil that he could make him some money playing the commodities markets. An investment pool had returned a lot of money to Good in recent weeks, and he wanted to share his fortune with Neil. Good explained that he would loan Neil $100,000 to invest. If the investment paid off, he got to keep the money. If it didn't, Neil didn't need to pay it back. Neil accepted the offer. How could he lose? "It was an incredibly sweet deal," he explained later.

"It was the Wild West in those days, and Ken Good was one of the high riders," Neil said. "He was worth tens of millions of dollars, and he enjoyed having people that he worked with participate in ventures with him. I know it sounds a little fishy, but I have heard this happened before."

Indeed, it had. Good made a point of it. "Frankly, this had been a modus operandi of mine for many years," he said. "It was a means of attracting and keeping loyal business associates in a form of compensation to them." Good handed out similar loans—anywhere from $10,000 to $350,000—to employees and friends. He once gave a secretary a new Corvette for doing good work. "Believe me, I never had trouble asking my secretary or my bookkeeper to work late when they could expect this kind of sharing in whatever success I might have."

A few days later, Good called Neil at the office. He had invested the $100,000 for Neil and the investment was paying off big. He offered Neil a choice: He could cash in or hope it went higher. Good, the consummate gambler, said he was staying with it. Neil followed suit. A few days later the investment was wiped out. Neil never repaid the loan.

By 1985, it was clear that JNB wasn't going to make money. Oil prices crashed, and this first wave of economic destruction wiped out hundreds of exploration firms that only months before had thrived. The Denver Petroleum Club—a grand, scarlet- carpeted monument to the age, where oil barons smoked cigars and toasted their prosperity—adopted the slogan: "Stay alive in '85." A huge mahogany showcase where plaques of member firms were displayed from one end of the room to the other became increasingly sparse as white-gloved stewards pried one dead firm's logo after another from the wall.

The fact that oil prices plummeted didn't make things any easier for JNB, but the truth of the matter was that oil prices hardly entered the equation. In its first months of operation, JNB had struck oil a few times, but never enough to be profitable. After those first successes, in five more years of drilling twenty-six wells, JNB never found oil. Not a drop. The partnership's early effort in the Powder River Basin, a veritable Shangri-La for other oil prospectors, failed. Somehow, JNB couldn't find the gushers that other oil companies were hitting. So they hunted around other parts of the Rocky Mountain West. They sank holes in Colorado, Wyoming, South Dakota. Nothing. They considered looking in Honduras and China, but finally put their hopes on Ohio. Before they were through, JNB acquired the rights to more than 500 potential wells. They drilled seven holes and came up dry every time. It may have been hard luck. But a puzzled official with the Ohio Department of Natural Resources wrote a memo about JNB's efforts in 1989 wondering why anyone had bothered with that part of the country. "The head of the Ohio oil and gas division says he doesn't know why anyone would want to dig in that region," the official wrote.

In April, Evans Nash took it upon himself to analyze oil industry literature and learned that the odds of finding another prospect were four times worse than they had thought. Further, he worried about the growing relationship between Good and Bush. "Neil wasn't the kind of guy to do something conniving. But somehow, I don't think he was so naive that he would get into something without knowing its ramifications," he said. "I had some concerns that weren't major but were enough for me to want to get out. I felt that Neil was fairly young and that he made some decisions that he wouldn't have if he were a little more experienced." So Nash sold his share of the company to Neil and Good and departed.

Along with oil, real estate began to show chinks in its armor. With the oil crash, people stopped moving to the state. Residential and commercial vacancy rates climbed and property values began a long, sickening plunge. In 1986, the government would rescind the Big Tax Break on commercial real estate, and the huge syndicates of investors would collapse. What had seemed an endless lava flow of cash would solidify and finally stop. Real estate developers would be left holding huge, empty, worthless buildings that they couldn't sell, and development companies would wither. But not Walters, and not Good. They would turn to Silverado, which, with Neil on the board, would help them continue to prosper. Neil Bush, in turn, would escape the jaws of the oil crash and bring home more pay than ever, thanks to Good and Walters.

6

The Incredible Perpetual Motion Machine

Physicists speak of certain natural laws of the universe, immutable rules by which all things exist. One of them is the law of conservation of energy, which has nothing to do with turning down the thermostat. It means that engines will stop running when the fuel is exhausted and fires will stop burning when the logs are spent.

Economics is not as exact a science as physics, but it is still true that banks are machines and money is the fuel that drives them. When an economy dries up and money runs low, the engine must slow down. In 1986, Denver's economic fuel was draining fast. It was becoming clear that the city had seriously overbuilt its downtown—nearly a third of total downtown office space was empty—and property values were plummeting. Commercial development of all kinds was grinding to a halt. In some ways these were mild economic harbingers compared with Marvin Davis' announcement in March that the annual Carousel Ball that had brought the stars to Denver wouldn't be held that year. More than anything, that told the story. Denver's big-money oil days were dying. The natural laws of the economic universe dictated that Silverado should slow down.

But Silverado's engine, driven by some invisible fuel, only moved faster—growing, reporting record profits and paying its executives huge sums of money when almost everyone else was scaling back. Most outsiders believed Silverado was the picture of ruddy health. In fact, it was in worse shape than it had ever been. Capital levels were dangerously low and loans were going bad so fast that the thrift could barely make new ones fast enough to cover up the losses. Foreclosed real estate taken back from borrowers who had stopped paying had soared during 1985 to ten times the level at the beginning of the year. Problem loans had quadrupled. Commercial centers and strip malls for which Silverado had lent money lay vacant or nearly vacant. Uncompleted condominium projects were ghost towns.

The physicist's law implies that the pistons of an engine encounter friction. That's why they stop when the fuel runs out. At a financial institution, one source of friction is supposed to be the board of directors. In the industry, the board is known as the first line of defense to protect taxpayers from marauding thrift managers; the loyalty of each director is sworn to the institution. It was a system—largely based on a strong sense of business ethics—that had worked for many years in the thrift industry. But Wise needed a board that would grease the wheels, not stand in his way.

With Neil on the board, that's what Wise got. In January 1986, just four months after Neil joined, vice chairman Vandapool wrote a memo to Wise (the same memo in which he praised Wise for transforming Silverado from a mess to a miracle). "Let's admit it," he wrote. "The board is a legal necessity, but you and Jim (majority stockholder W. James

Metz) control the company and you control the directors. You know it and they know it. The (outside) directors simply ratify our actions and decisions. Why meet monthly? Why spend significant time and money to provide ten directors with information that the majority of them don't or won't comprehend?"

The entire board seemed ready to acknowledge that their wisdom was inferior to that of Silverado's management. "I don't think anybody on that board of directors had a sophisticated knowledge of those transactions," director Florian Barth said in 1989. "Most of the information was given to us already prepared. The real estate transactions we were getting involved in all looked pretty good when you wrote them up. Basically, what we looked at were deals that had already been approved by the loan committee. Frankly, I'd never seen (those kinds of) transactions. It certainly could be unorthodox, but unorthodoxy doesn't mean it's wrong."

Wise wasn't entirely responsible for assembling the collection of directors who sat around the long conference table in the Skydeck each month. Indeed, the board had come together haphazardly over the decades of Silverado's evolution. Marjorie Page, for instance, a clerk and recorder of a suburban county, joined in 1966 when Silverado was still the tiny Circle Savings. She had come up in the days when sitting on the board of a thrift was more like being a member of the Lions Club; it was a status symbol of sorts, more social than business. At that time, thrifts didn't do a lot that could be criticized, so there wasn't much for a board member to be critical of. By the time Circle had become Silverado, she was a grandmotherly figure who by her own admission didn't understand most of the deals Silverado put together. What's more, she was awed by Wise, whom she regarded as "a brilliant young man with a lot of business sense." She figured Silverado's executives knew how to run their business and it was her job to stay out of the way. In one board meeting, apparently confused by the transaction detailed in her director's report, she leaned over to Bob Lewis and whispered, "Is this loan okay to approve?"

The words might have come from any of them. The board unanimously approved every transaction Wise put before it. Only once, in 1987, did one director finally raise his voice in a single defiant vote. By then it was too late.

The directors had little in common other than the awe-inspired belief that Wise and his executives knew what was best. Barth, who came from Mile High's board of directors, was an auto dealer who'd made his money selling expensive cars to Denver's growing rich. Richard Bunchman, whom Wise asked to join when Silverado bought the thrift where he was a director in 1983, owned a little real estate company in the mountain resort town of Breckenridge. Richard Vitkus, a sad-looking lawyer for Beatrice Foods Company, also joined in 1983 when Wise asked him to the board. Diane Ingels, who owned and ran her own real estate companies, joined in January 1985.

These people weren't stupid. But they weren't experts in thrift operations either. Wise exploited their ignorance with dazzling presentations that made even the most nefarious transaction look good. He piled reams of documents into beautifully bound directors' reports that often reached hundreds of pages. Because the directors usually got the reports only a day—two days in a good month—before the board meeting, most of them didn't even read the material. But it looked great.

Wise solicited experts—lawyers and accountants—to verify the legitimacy of the deals. Lewis spun numbers like silk, weaving them into great webs that most of the directors later said were so complicated they didn't know what to think—other than to be impressed. "Frankly, in all the meetings I ever attended, I have never seen anything done as completely as it was done by Michael Wise and the executive staff at Silverado," Barth told Congress in 1990, explaining why the board so vehemently believed in Silverado's management. With all the documentation we had . . . through explanation by people who were very expert, knowing what their focus was and how they put their product on the table, it would appear from all evidence that Silverado was not in any trouble."

Just before officially taking his new Silverado job, Neil met in Silverado's board room with Wise and his vice chairmen, Richard Vandapool and Bob Lewis. For all practical purposes, Neil had accepted the offer to become a Silverado director. But there were some formalities to deal with. It's customary for new directors of most businesses to peruse financial statements and talk to management. It's meant to be an opportunity for a director to see firsthand what he or she is getting into and, if it comes to that, backing out if the situation looks bad. In this case, management did all the talking.

Seated around the conference table, the executives took turns offering evidence of Silverado's excellent condition. Neil was mesmerized. "I don't remember what assurances I received that gave me the impression Silverado was in good shape," he told government investigators in December 1989. "To be totally honest with you, I'm not sure I could have formed an opinion at the time. I wasn't familiar with savings and loan financials." During an interview several months later, he tried again to recall what it was that had made him believe Silverado was in good shape. "I was impressed by the thoroughness of those guys. And I was impressed by what they presented as a solid financial institution."

Neil said later he realized at his first board meeting that Silverado was "in serious trouble. It became evident to me that Silverado was having some problems. But I'm the kind of guy—I get married, I get married for life. I don't think they deceived me. I don't think they realized themselves the extent of the problems."

Neil plunged in with obvious relish. On days when the board met, Neil sometimes ambled among the desks in the penthouse before mounting the stairway to the Skydeck, where board meetings were held. He waved to people he recognized and shook hands, politician-style.

In the glass-walled board room of the Skydeck, Neil applied himself to his job. He made it a point to raise questions despite the fact—as he later admitted—that he would "never claim to have fully understood everything that took place" in Silverado's board room.

Soon, Neil began reaping the benefits of his new job. In January he replaced his $289,000 mortgage from World Savings with a $300,000 loan from Silverado that gave him a two percent break on the interest rate. And he attended charity galas that Silverado had begun to take an interest in, including one for which Silverado paid $30,000 to benefit a child abuse organization called Hope for the Children. It was staged under a lilac dusk on the hedged estate of Denver real estate investor John Dick, whose gothic mansion rose over acres of closely clipped lawn. "This thing was really something," recalled a guest who sat at Neil's table. "All the celebrities were there. It was like Hollywood had come to Denver. Neil and his wife really seemed to enjoy that sort of thing. I remember wondering whether he knew he was being used as window-dressing at Silverado. People talked about it behind his back. But he seemed to enjoy himself, so I didn't worry about it."

At the same party, Walters and Good engaged in a battle of one-upmanship at the auction table, where guests bid against one another for prizes, the proceeds going to charity. The grand prize was a two-week trip to John Dick's multi-million-dollar 16th century manor house on the Isle of Jersey in the English Channel. Dick was one of a handful of

Americans allowed to purchase land on the tiny, castle-dotted island, an exclusive destination for European jet-setters. Each year, the island's government allowed five very rich foreigners who could afford a $4 million piece of land to purchase property. It was a way to attract the wealthiest people in the world to support its banking-based economy. Dick bought a 250-acre lushly wooded estate and the title "Seignior of St. John's" that went with it. He liked to entertain at his castle and invited guests—including Walters (who was later accused of spiriting $20 million to the island's banks, out of the reach of bankruptcy courts trying to get his assets) and Silverado director Diane Ingels—to enjoy the beaches, tennis courts and narrow country lanes winding through fields of lavender. It was a vacation worth paying for.

Walters and Good didn't need to pay. They could have gone any time they wanted. Nonetheless, they bid furiously against each other, calling out higher figures in rapid succession until the auctioneer finally extracted $15,000 from Good, and Walters would go no higher. Good never took the trip.

Despite the good times, Wise was presented in early 1986 with serious problems that threatened the future of his institution. First, regulators were raising "concerns." To most people, concerns are relatively minor irritations, life's headaches. But regulators speak in muted, bureaucratic language. To them, a concern is a problem of herculean proportions. Arcing electrical wires in a kerosene factory are a concern. The regulators called a meeting on January 3, 1986. Wise, Lewis and Vandapool filed into the room, and the examiners slapped on the table the results of an examination performed the previous November. An astonishing 66 percent of Silverado's loan portfolio was concentrated in high-risk loans. More than 22 percent of its loans were already bad. Based on the report, it looked as if Silverado had lost $10 million in 1985 when the thrift reported a $12 million profit.

Further, it appeared Silverado was hiding its bad loans by simply not reporting them on required forms, and capital again was dangerously low.

Wise and Lewis had tried to argue in a seventy-three-page letter that the examiners' conclusions were wrong. The examiners didn't buy it. They grilled Silverado management about everything from its loan policies to its practice of awarding big bonuses to senior executives when the thrift was doing so poorly. On February 20, they lowered the boom, their first restrictive action against Silverado. Among other things, the regulators demanded that Silverado immediately recognize the losses that were clearly on the books and ordered management to report every three months with an assessment of its loan underwriting and loan monitoring system. Further, they said Silverado must raise its capital to 5 percent of assets by June 30 or face regulatory action.

The second problem facing Wise was the 1985 audit by Silverado's outside accounting firm, Ernst & Whinney. Every financial institution must submit its financial statements to the scrutiny of a certified public accounting firm. Accountants are supposed to keep managers in line by ensuring that all profits and losses are properly accounted for. For three years running, Ernst & Whinney had regarded Silverado's claims of prosperity with growing skepticism. Still, the firm had issued clean opinions, though it wrote up warnings to Silverado's management. In 1985, however, Silverado's problems were too big to ignore. Silverado handed over its financial statements showing a $12 million profit. But as Ernst & Whinney accountants waded into the mountains of paperwork, they found so many bad loans that Silverado had either ignored or tried to hide that they forced the thrift to recognize $40 million in loan losses.

That didn't sit well with Silverado's management, partly because it meant they would have to show a $15 million loss for the year and partly because senior executives would have

Neil at a mid-1980s Republican rally in Denver.

Neil and Sharon at a party.

Neil and Sharon stumping for George in New Orleans.

Neil's family at the unveiling of his father's portrait.

Neil and Sharon at GOP fundraiser.

Neil Bush at his office at JNB Exploration.

Michael Wise turned Mile High Savings into Silverado.

Headquarters of Mile High Savings before Wise took over.

Walters (left) with model of proposed Silverado building.

Ken Good, in his office, wanted to be Denver's richest man.

Ken Good testifying before the House Banking Committee.

Bill Walters played black jack for $50,000 a hand in Vegas.

Ken Good and friend at Rolls Royce club gathering.

Neil celebrating his father's victory November 8, 1988.

Federal Marshals taking over Silverado in December, 1988.

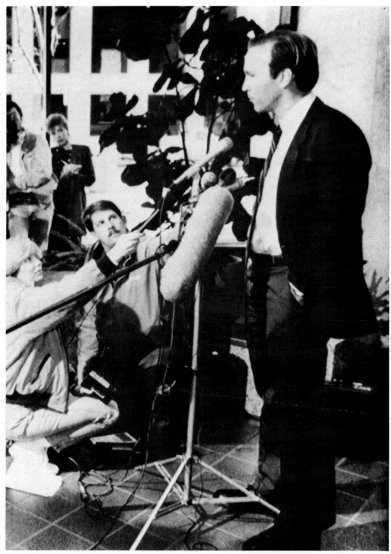

Neil at a 1990 press conference denying any wrongdoing.

to forgo huge bonuses based on the reported record profit. Adding to the predicament, the 1985 loss would preclude Silverado from paying dividends on its preferred stock. A clause in the stock sales agreement said that if Silverado failed to pay dividends for four consecutive quarters, the preferred shareholders could take over the thrift. Wise and Metz would lose control if they didn't pay dividends by June 30.

Yet another disaster was looming. Both Wise and Metz had taken out huge loans to buy Silverado stock. Metz's $2.5 million loan at United Bank of Denver was due June 30, and he didn't have the money to pay it. United refused to extend the loan, and no other bank would make him a new loan collateralized with Silverado shares. If he didn't pay by the deadline, United could foreclose, taking Metz's stock and consequently his ownership in the thrift. Likewise, Wise owed Walters' Cherry Creek National Bank $1.75 million for his Silverado stock.

June 30 was a triple witching hour. Silverado needed capital to get regulators off its back. It needed to pay dividends to fend off preferred shareholders. And Metz and Wise needed cash to pay their loans. All by June 30.

Lewis put his head to the problem and came up with an intricate solution to all three ills. Using a line of credit from Silverado, a Silverado real estate subsidiary would pay $16.5 million to buy raw land from Walters. The land was worth only a fraction of that price, but Silverado had no plans to develop the property. Instead, Walters would buy back the property at a future date. The transactions were simply a way to allow money and assets to change hands. At the same time Silverado bought the land, the thrift would loan $18.5 million to Walters for a shopping mall development called the Galleria. The Galleria mall was to be the crown jewel in Walters' commercial real estate empire, one of the largest and most elaborate shopping malls in the state, despite the alarming vacancy rate in the malls that already crowded Southeast Denver. Walters would use $7 million of the loan to buy stock in a new holding company—Silverado Financial Corp.—that Silverado would create at the precise moment the deal was put into motion. As soon as Walters bought the stock, Silverado would pay him $1.5 million in dividends on the stock he had just purchased with Silverado money.

At the June board meeting, the deal was unanimously approved, and the transaction's machinery whirred into life. With the money Walters paid for his stock, Wise and Metz paid off their loans. In effect, they had taken Silverado money to pay their own debts, which is illegal when the amount exceeds $100,000. But the money had taken a circuitous route, making the payment appear legitimate. The remainder of the cash and the real estate Silverado bought from Walters was used to bolster capital. And by forming a new holding company, the old Silverado stock with the clause allowing preferred shareholders to take over was replaced by new shares that didn't have a takeover clause. The triple witch was defeated.

Lewis received a $117,000 bonus for his work. Walters later defaulted on the $18.5 million loan. He also never bought back the real estate, leaving Silverado to absorb the loss. Metz and Wise never repaid the $4.25 million they used to pay their personal debts.

That same month, Wise borrowed $847,710 for a $1 million mansion in the Country Club neighborhood. It was a magnificent Tudor with stately elms gracing the expansive lot at one of Denver's most exclusive addresses. Wise had tried to convince regulators to let Silverado pay for the house. But when they refused, he took out the loan, which charged him annual interest of 8.35 percent at a time when other institutions were charging 10 to 11 percent for similar loans. The terms of the loan didn't require Wise to make regular interest payments.

At the June board meeting, Neil voted to approve the complex deal along with the rest of the directors, despite the fact that Walters had invested in his company and despite the fact that Neil apparently had agreed to abstain from all votes concerning the developer. When Neil joined the board in August 1985, Wise wrote a letter to Silverado's preferred shareholders dated July 15, 1985. "In reviewing Neil's business relationships, we have learned his business interests include associations with Bill L. Walters and Kenneth M. Good," Wise wrote. "For his part, Neil has agreed to abstain from any board considerations regarding Silverado's relations with Mr. Walters or Mr. Good, and Neil has further agreed he will not participate in any board actions relating to preferred stock or preferred stockholders."

The letter has been the subject of some mystery. Neil claims he never made such an agreement and never saw the letter, which is signed by Wise. Some of the other directors later told government attorneys that they had seen the letter but still later recanted and said they couldn't recall having seen it. If there was an agreement, Neil didn't stick to it very long. At his first board meeting in September, he did just what he was supposedly forbidden to do. He voted to approve stock dividends to Silverado's preferred shareholders, which included Good and Walters.

The letter notwithstanding, by mid 1986 Neil was immersed in deep conflicts of interest between his loyalties to Silverado and to Walters and Good. In addition to the $150,000 Walters had initially sunk into JNB, Walters' Cherry Creek National Bank had extended Neil nearly $2 million in loans and lines of credit. Further, Good had told Neil that he was going to pump $5 million into JNB to keep it alive and running.

Good said he would use the $5 million to buy 80 percent of JNB and fold the company into his new Florida-based real estate company, Gulfstream Land & Development Corp. It was the only way he could continue to fund JNB. The developer had nearly broken himself in the acquisition of Gulfstream earlier in the year. The $250 million purchase capped an orgy of Florida real estate acquisitions that totaled $525 million. Good had flown from banker to banker until he and his negotiators were reduced to "flipping through the Yellow Pages looking for S&Ls we hadn't called on yet," one of the negotiators said later, describing the deal's last days. The orgy left Good with almost no cash and up to his eyes in bank and junk bond debt. He was so leveraged that the combined cash flow of his companies couldn't keep up. As Neil said later, Good was "strapped." But by absorbing JNB and other companies he owned into Gulfstream, Good told Neil he could keep the money coming in.

Under his proposed arrangement with Neil, Good planned to pump $5 million into JNB. Part of the money would go to pay off loans Bush had at Walters' Cherry Creek National Bank. Already Neil relied on Good's contributions to "maintain our overhead and maintain operation and activities," Neil said in 1990. Without Good, he would have been out of a job. Neil agreed that it seemed the best thing to do, so they set the machinery in motion to do the deal.

Despite all that, Neil didn't believe he had any conflicts of interest. At the June board meeting, after voting on the Walters transactions, Neil and the other directors received a standard "Acknowledgement of Conflicts of Interest and Code of Conduct" form. It's a common procedure for directors at any financial institution to fill one out each year. The form asks directors to write down any relationship that might "create or appear to create" a conflict with his or her activities as a director. Walters and Good were two of Silverado's biggest borrowers. Neil owed Walters' Cherry Creek National Bank $2 million for JNB expenses plus a $20,000 line of credit Neil took out for personal use. He owed virtual fealty to Good for keeping the lights on at JNB. But when Neil put his pen to the conflict form, he wrote in the space provided, "None."

Neil later claimed that the money Walters and Good put into JNB never entered his mind as he approved $106 million in loans to Walters, all of which eventually went bad. A case can be made that Neil's state of mind didn't matter. Even if he had voted against the Walters transactions, the deals would likely have gone through anyway. After all, each transaction was unanimously approved by the board. Clearly, Neil didn't cause Silverado to do the deals. He just didn't create any friction.

Regulators, however, argued that a single vote could have made a huge difference in Silverado's board by breaking its herd mentality and creating a sense of critical independence. In any case, Neil's conflict between his own interests and Silverado's with respect to Walters took another step in October 1986. Walters wanted out of JNB. Neil's partnership was at the height of its non-success, but that apparently wasn't the reason Walters wanted to ditch his share. "Oh, that had nothing to do with it," a friend said. "He didn't pay any attention to the investment. Bill found out Ken was dating his wife." It was true. Ken Good, a helpless philanderer by his own account, couldn't resist Walters' wife, Mary Lou, and Walters didn't want anything more to do with the man. "It was a matter of face," the friend said. When divorce proceedings started, Good—who had been through a divorce himself—added insult to injury by advising Mary Lou on how Walters would try to hide assets from her. Testifying before an administrative law judge in 1990, Neil put it this way: "This is a little touchy because it involves a personal matter . . . Bill Walters got a divorce. Ken Good got involved in that divorce and on the wrong side of the divorce, and so Ken Good and Bill Walters weren't likely to become or stay partners for very long." Walters' friend was more blunt: "Bill was pissed." The developer apparently recovered quickly, however, and married his secretary less than a year later.

Walters sold his share of the business to Neil and Good for his original $150,000 investment. JNB didn't have that much money on hand, so the company cut Walters a check for $50,000, and Walters said they could owe him the extra $100,000. It was never repaid. The fact that Walters invested at all in JNB established a relationship between Neil and the real estate developer that amounted to "pure financial self-interest," concluded ethics expert Edward Conry, who testified for the government at Neil's administrative hearing in 1990. But if Walters had forced Neil and his partners to pay the $100,000, it could have ended JNB's existence at almost any time, Conry said, and the loan became leverage that rendered Neil "unable to make impartial judgments where the interests of Mr. Walters were involved."

In early November 1986, at the bidding of Good's attorneys, Neil sent a letter to Mike Wise asking Silverado to extend a $900,000 line of credit to one of Good's companies, Good International Inc. The credit line was meant to help Good show the government of Argentina that the developer had enough financial wherewithal to do business in the country, Neil said in the letter. He never mentioned—not to Wise, not to executives who assembled the deal, not to the board—that the company was formed expressly to fund Bush's plan to take JNB's exploration efforts into Argentina. Bush abstained, but the board approved the line of credit, despite the fact that Good couldn't put up any collateral. "If I would have had that information, I might not have even prepared the memo," said the Silverado executive who recommended that the credit line be extended.

Less than a month later, at the November 24 board meeting, Wise informed the directors that Good was threatening to default on a $31 million loan Silverado had given him for a chunk of prairie south of Denver. Good had paid a visit to Silverado Center One and taken the elevator to the Skydeck to meet with Mike Wise and Bob Lewis. His beard was short. "I have a problem," he said. "And you have a problem."

Good had planned to sell the property that collateralized the loan and pay back the $31 million from his proceeds. But now, Good couldn't even sell the property, much less recover the $31 million. "It hasn't sold," he told them, "and based on the way things look in the market, I don't think it will sell." He didn't want Silverado to foreclose, so he was ready to deal. He offered to pay $3 million up front if Silverado would release the collateral and some $11.5 million in personal guarantees.

When the board met to discuss the problem, Neil said nothing about Good's plan to put $5 million into JNB, money that might have gone toward the loan. The matter was put off until December. Again, Neil sat silently as his fellow directors approved the deal. Good's collateral was released, and the developer defaulted. Silverado ate the loss.

Perhaps in a gesture of appreciation, Good awarded Neil a $45,000 pay raise and a $22,000 bonus at JNB, bringing his total yearly income from the oil company to $142,000.

Wise also benefited from Good in the restructuring. At the same time that Silverado released Good's collateral and personal guarantees, Wise bought from Good $14 million in Silverado stock for $100,000 in cash and $2.9 million in nonrecourse notes.

As the end of 1986 approached, Silverado's management worked furiously to boost profits, hoping to surpass a target of $8 million in earnings for the year. For every extra dollar the thrift earned beyond its target, executives would receive bonuses.

Loans continued to go bad at an astonishing rate. But Lewis had figured out a way to get rid of bad loans while increasing capital at the same time, allowing Silverado to make more new loans and grow faster. It was financial alchemy. Bad loans equal losses and depleted capital. It's another of the financial world's natural laws, as constant as gravity. But deregulation warped the universe, leaving little holes in space where the laws could be disobeyed. One of the holes was that savings and loans could count certain investments among their capital reserves. Another was looser accounting rules regarding the way thrifts could record loan losses on their books. Lewis saw a way to put the two together.

What he did was simple, really. He developed a program based on an old political principle: I'll scratch your back if you scratch mine. The program was called Quid Pro Quo, this for that. Under the program, Silverado would lend money to real estate developers who were hard up for cash. In return, the developers would use some of the money to buy Silverado stock or to purchase bad loans from Silverado. When they bought stock, it boosted Silverado's capital level. When they bought bad loans, the thrift's books were cleaned up, or so the theory went.

The program seemed perfectly legitimate on the surface, but in reality, it was just a shell game. The deals did nothing to make Silverado healthier; it just looked that way. Since the stock was bought with Silverado's own cash (in the form of extra loan money), the transactions did nothing to boost capital. Silverado simply recorded the sales as though new cash were coming into the thrift. Likewise, the bad loans developers bought with Silverado money only put off the day of reckoning. The thrift got rid of a bad loan, but since it had to inflate the new loan far beyond the value of the property, the new loan was likely to go sour some time in the future. When it did, Silverado would be stuck with a bigger loss than it had before.

In a variation on the Quid Pro Quo program, Lewis dumped all the thrift's bad loans, all its foreclosed real estate, all its souring investments along with loans that were still performing into a pile called the loan pool. Lewis reasoned that all the loans together really were one big asset, not hundreds of individual ones. And since individual loans didn't exist in the pool, Lewis further reasoned that the nonperforming loans no longer had to be accounted for on Silverado's books. That meant millions in potential losses simply didn't exist anymore as far as Silverado was concerned.

What's more, Lewis figured Silverado could slice the pool into little pieces, which could be sold like bonds. Essentially, Lewis had reinvented Wall Street's mortgage-backed security, only this time a thrift was doing it, not the New York investment houses. By the mid '80s, Wall Street firms were trading wildly sophisticated mortgage investments, all derived from big pools of loans disgorged by thrifts across the country. The New York houses made fortunes dealing in the mortgage paper, and they would buy anything a thrift had to offer because there was always another thrift out there willing to buy.

But there is an exception to every rule. Wall Street would have nothing to do with Silverado's paper. Lewis tried to sell a $200 million piece of the loan pool to Drexel Burnham Lambert. Drexel—home to Michael Milken, creator of junk bonds, the house that was trading perhaps more thrift paper than any other Wall Street firm—wouldn't touch it. In the words of Henry Gonzalez, a Democratic congressman from Texas, "Even the junk yard dogs would have no part of this toxic pool."

This might have presented a problem, but Silverado had already figured out how to make a market for its trash: force it on borrowers as a condition for getting a loan. Real estate developers simply got a slightly bigger loan from Silverado than they had asked for and used the extra cash to buy loan pool securities. Silverado used the cash from the sale to boost its capital reserve, even though it had come from the institution to begin with. In reality, Silverado had no more capital than before. But it looked that way, and that's what mattered.

To do these deals, Silverado needed the cooperation of real estate appraisers. An appraiser's report on the value of a property is required for every real estate loan a thrift makes. Typically, thrifts use the appraisal to calculate how much they will lend on a piece of property. Usually, thrifts will lend 80 percent of a property's value to cover itself in case the loan goes bad or property values fall. Silverado often lent 100 percent of the appraised value. Sometimes it didn't even bother to get an appraisal, or it determined the amount of money it would loan before having the property appraised.

At the time, real estate appraisers were entirely unregulated, and a segment of the industry specialized in inflated appraisals. They were the cleverest and the most unscrupulous of the trade. They were also the ones who made the most money. Financial institutions pay the appraiser's fee, and as a rule, the higher the appraisal, the more the institution likes it and the more likely it is to hire that appraiser again.

Armed with a stable of right-thinking appraisers, its Quid Pro Quo program and the loan pool, Silverado went on a loan hunt. With the help of loan brokers in twenty-five cities across the country, Silverado's loan department worked overtime scouring the landscape for more than a quarter of a billion dollars in loans to blast its bottom line through the roof. The institution apparently didn't care whether the loans would be profitable investments. It wanted fees and it wanted developers desperate enough to agree to Silverado's terms. "Silverado needed these transactions in order to appear healthy, to conceal nonperforming assets, to artificially boost net worth and to increase fee income at year end," the

Federal Deposit Insurance Corp. said in its $200 million gross negligence lawsuit against Silverado. "These short-term gains were achieved at a devastating cost to the association."

In a special board meeting at the end of December, Silverado's executive loan officers took turns offering thirteen deals to Silverado's board, which unanimously approved them all. In each case, Silverado lent more than the property was worth. And in each case, the loan went bad within two years.

There was a $30.5 million loan for a twenty-seven-story Manhattan apartment co-op that was losing money (the borrower used half the money to buy Silverado stock); a $4.65 million loan for an apartment building in Venice Beach in West Los Angeles; $24.5 million for the Los Angeles Sports Club; a $16 million land development loan on 334 acres in Fort Worth; a $14.5 million loan on 418 acres in Camarillo, California; $20 million for a department store in San Antonio. The list went on.

In some cases, Silverado simply restructured existing loans. For instance, one real estate developer in Denver stopped paying on his $4.4 million loan for a warehouse. Instead of foreclosing, Silverado gave him a new $32 million loan, despite the fact that the warehouse had been empty for two years. The developer used $2 million of that to buy Silverado stock. Silverado booked $750,000 in fees.

In another case, a real estate partnership had tried unsuccessfully to get a $15 million loan to renovate a gutted, uninhabitable building in downtown Denver. Two dozen banks and thrifts had rejected the application. Silverado loaned the partnership $22 million based on an appraisal that calculated the value of air rights above the building according to real estate values in New York City. The appraiser never considered that Denver's downtown vacancy rate was the highest in the nation, rendering air rights virtually worthless. The developer used $3.75 million to buy a bad loan from

Silverado and another $1.25 million to purchase Silverado stock. Silverado collected a $750,000 fee from the loan.

Those loans, however, were mere trifles compared with the thrift's last and most complicated transaction of the year, a labyrinthine deal with Bill Walters. Silverado expanded the $18.5 million loan it had made to Walters earlier in the year to $44 million. Walters used $6 million of the money to buy Silverado stock. Silverado didn't seem to care whether it got paid back; the loan was nonrecourse, meaning that Silverado had no way of recovering the money. Silverado didn't charge him points or fees and didn't update its year-old appraisal on the property, despite the fact that the real estate market all over Denver had fallen through the floor. None of the loan funds were budgeted for construction or development of the mall.

At the same time, Silverado bought from Walters an undeveloped city block in downtown Denver for $33.9 million. (Walters had bought it for $22.5 million just fourteen months before, when the real estate market was considerably better than it was in late 1986.) Walters must have been glad to get rid of the property. He had bought it in 1985 from a Texas real estate developer who had snapped it up during the building boom of the early 1980s. But when the market began to fall, the developer sold it to Walters for $200 a square foot. Walters thought he was getting a good deal at the time, but the empty block was sinking in value as downtown vacancy rates soared. If he couldn't get rid of it, he would have been stuck with a $200-a- square-foot liability. But Silverado took it off his hands for $300 a square foot. Walters used $5.7 million of the cash Silverado paid to buy 570,000 shares of the thrift's stock.

Silverado also bought from Walters a gutted, abandoned building in downtown Denver. The thrift paid $20.4 million for the property, and Walters used $8.3 million of it to buy more stock. There was little if any redeeming value in the transaction for Silverado. But Walters said he would build a magnificent skyscraper on the site, with pink Spanish marble, garden terraces and expansive skylights. It would be the most distinctive building in downtown Denver, Walters said. And it would be Silverado's new headquarters. The transaction included a promise for a ten-year Silverado lease in the building, which Walters would design and build. "The property will be a superior location for Silverado's corporate headquarters in the 1990s," the papers said. Wise even worked in a deal in which Walters would pay the balance of Silverado's lease at the old building if the thrift could move in before the old lease expired.

The series of transactions gave Silverado $20 million in new capital. Walters walked away with $19 million in cash, which he never repaid. Plus, he booked a profit from the land sales and had two fewer troubled properties to worry about.

The board approved the transactions despite the fact that the going downtown lease rate was just $13 a square foot and the deal needed at least $22 a square foot to break even. Worse, the building frenzy of the early '80s had produced almost 7 million square feet of office space more than Denver companies could rent. By the middle of 1986, companies were moving out at the rate of 1.2 million square feet a year. The board knew this. It was in the loan presentation. But Wise said the market would come back. And they believed him.

The year-end deals generated so much fee income that Silverado reported a $15 million profit for the year, well in excess of the $8 million target. Regulators later calculated that Silverado actually lost $15 million. Based on the windfall, Wise, Lewis, Vandapool and Russell Murray, Silverado's head of commercial lending, gave themselves bonuses totaling $2.3 million. Wise alone made more than sixteen of the top-paid executives at two of Denver's biggest commercial banks combined.

At the year's close, Bill Walters married his secretary, Jacqueline Brown. "It was a dream celebration," a Denver society columnist wrote. "Sentimental, tender, romantic, the kind reserved for princes and princesses—or kings and queens." More than four hundred people attended the reception following the wedding, "a gold and white extravaganza where the luminaries gathered amid a riot of crystal, twinkling lights and fantasy mannequins." A guest sighed: "It was more glamorous and a bigger production than the Carousel Ball." Who cared if Marvin Davis had left town? Who cared whether the economy was in the tank? They were rich. What else in the world mattered?

7

God's Little Acre

Larry Mizel drove a white Rolls Royce, which seems to say something about the man. He possessed a Jay Gatsby smoothness; he was a handshaker, an introducer. Influence was his game, and he devoted as much energy to fostering relationships with politicians and powerful business leaders as he did to making his M.D.C. Holdings Inc. the nation's fifth-largest home builder. He habitually worked eighteen-hour days, which he often ended by jetting off to parties held by the latest and greatest in business and politics. "He will visit two or three cocktail parties a night, and they may not all be in Colorado," an associate said. "Larry goes at a rate of 100 miles per hour. Larry loves to make contacts."

He also was a rich man—estimates put his fortune at $35 million—who saw to it that political candidates for offices from county commissioner to president were the beneficiaries of his largesse. He and his wife personally gave $117,300 to sixty- two candidates, and he raised millions more through fund raisers (usually for the Republican party) that consistently drew the nation's highest dignitaries. In 1986 he chaired the most successful political fund raiser in Colorado history, raising $1 million at a luncheon attended by President Ronald Reagan. Mizel gave, he said, because "I believe in good government."

But he also was a man who knew how to extract a return on his money. Self-made in every sense, he long ago had taught himself the lessons of capitalism. The grandchild of Russian immigrants and the son of a salvage-yard boss and sometime oil wildcatter in Tulsa, Oklahoma, Mizel went into business for himself before he could drive. As a kid, he cold-called numbers in his mother's address book, pitching magazine subscriptions and sending his mother out to collect the money. He later engineered with his brother a cigarette vending machine route. At 16, he cleaned up used cars from his father's salvage lot and advertised them in the Tulsa paper, making $100 or $200 a shot.

He was 24 when he came to Colorado for law school at the University of Denver. In his first year, he invested an $18,000 inheritance in the construction of a ninety-six-unit apartment building fittingly called The de Medici. "I was a better builder than a student," he explained.

A year later he was in another apartment deal, The Corsican, then another. Five years out of law school, in 1972, Mizel started Mizel Development Corp. (later condensed to M.D.C. Holdings Inc.) with Emil Hecht, an accountant and survivor of Hitler's concentration camps. They didn't start with much, just $20,000 and a stake in ten acres of land. At first the company built apartments on spec and managed buildings, a small operation by later standards. In 1974, M.D.C. went public on Denver's notorious penny stock market, raising $500,000. Before long it was building condominiums and houses for the waves of people who washed into Denver, and M.D.C. began to swell.

In 1982, Mizel's company was standing at the foot of a great opportunity. M.D.C. was still just a local home builder, but Mizel wanted more. Like manna from heaven, financial deregulation was laid at his feet.

The first gift was Michael Milken's junk bonds. Junk wasn't technically a product of deregulation. Rather, it had sprung from Milken's "monster brain," as one of his friends called it, amid Wall Street's helter-skelter environment in the 1980s, which was created in part by deregulation.

Milken was making corporate behemoths out of ordinary businesses. Companies that weren't big enough or strong enough to raise money through bonds rated by major investment houses got Milken's help. He could raise millions in a week issuing bonds considered too risky to be rated. Working from his X-shaped desk on the fourth-floor trading room of Drexel Burnham Lambert's offices on Wilshire Boulevard in Beverly Hills, Milken raised almost $100 billion between 1977 and 1989. Milken was a financial Ponce de Leon and his Beverly Hills office a spring that promised eternal riches.

In 1983, Mizel went to the fountain and drank. By 1986, Milken had raised $700 million for M.D.C., and the company spread like an ivy across the nation, to Arizona, Georgia, Florida, California and Washington, D.C.

Mizel became a Milken groupie, one of the privileged few who entered the junk-bond king's inner circle. He is said to have become good friends with Milken, and in 1985 he founded a junk bond lobbying group called Alliance for Capital Access to keep Congress from fiddling with the system that had made him a wealthy man.

The second gift to Mizel was savings and loans. About the time Mizel went to Milken, he became fascinated by thrifts. These newly deregulated institutions had money to spend, money to invest—money that could make his company grow.

He directed M.D.C. to acquire an interest in Denver's Columbia Savings, his first dabble in thrift ownership. He apparently liked what he saw because M.D.C. quickly bought shares in San Diego's Imperial Savings and Los Angeles giant FarWest Financial, both huge customers of Drexel's junk bonds. "As a home builder, M.D.C. was familiar with the changes in regulations governing the thrift industry adopted in the early 1980s," he would later write. "As M.D.C. management observed the rapid growth and high reported profits of many thrifts, it concluded that the industry presented good investment opportunities."

Then, in 1984, he found Silverado in his own back yard. Richard Schierburg and Steve Arent, who ran Silverado's newly formed real estate subsidiary, approached M.D.C. with a deal. They would buy real estate from M.D.C. and M.D.C. would buy Silverado stock. The deal was beautiful in its simplicity and its symbiosis. By taking land from M.D.C., Silverado took from the home builder the risk of holding large amounts of undeveloped real estate, whose price could plummet at any moment. Silverado also helped M.D.C. book a profit on land sales. On the other side of the coin, M.D.C. boosted Silverado's net worth by purchasing Silverado stock, allowing the thrift to continue its explosive growth. M.D.C. got an added bonus in the form of guaranteed dividends, which paid a minimum 10.5 percent a year. If Silverado failed to pay four consecutive dividends, Mizel could take control of the thrift.

But there was more. Mizel found that savings and loans could act like stables for real estate. By passing parcels of land from one thrift to the next, everyone in the chain could make money as they inflated prices along the way.

The biggest players in Mizel's chain were Silverado and Charles Keating's Lincoln Savings and Loan in Irvine, California. Keating, a major contributor to Mizel's junk bond lobbying group, gave M.D.C. a $75 million line of credit from Lincoln, and the two companies swapped real estate. For instance, a Lincoln subsidiary, AMCOR, bought 6,000 undeveloped home sites from M.D.C., and M.D.C. bought nearly 4,000 from AMCOR. No money changed hands, but both companies booked a profit.

Silverado, Lincoln and M.D.C. juggled real estate like hot potatoes. AMCOR, the real estate subsidiary of Lincoln Savings, bought 2,900 acres of saguaro cactus and bullet-scarred beer cans in the Arizona desert near the dust-choked stream bed of the Santa Cruz River. M.D.C. bought some of the land for a higher price, allowing AMCOR to book a profit. Three months later Silverado-Elektra, the real estate subsidiary of Silverado, bought the same land for more than four times its original price, allowing M.D.C. to book a profit. Completing the cycle, Silverado-Elektra sold the property to a Nevada-based development firm called R.A. Homes, which regulators said was a front for Lincoln Savings.

Another deal in Southern California worked the same way. M.D.C. sold 324 acres known as Rancho Acacia to Silverado for $13.3 million. Six months later, M.D.C. bought the land back for $17 million. Five months after that, M.D.C. sold the land to another Lincoln front, Hamilton Homes, for $14.9 million. The same day, Lincoln sold M.D.C. 964 acres of doomed real estate in Arizona.

These were sweet relationships for Mizel. Regulators said deals with Silverado accounted for as much as 80 percent of M.D.C.'s profits in 1984 and 1985. By 1985 the company was one of the nation's great real estate powers. Its stock, having outgrown the penny market, was traded on the New York Stock Exchange, and it sold more than 2,400 homes with predictions of doubling that figure the following year, compelling Forbes to proclaim M.D.C. the fastest-growing home builder in the country. Mizel would take home $1.1 million in salary and bonuses.

By 1986, Mizel's thrift and political connections were at their peak, and his company was about to embark on a scheme that would erupt four years later as the biggest political scandal in Colorado history.

It was summer of 1986. Three men gathered in the office of David Mandarich on the sixth floor of M.D.C.'s headquarters. Mandarich was M.D.C.'s president and Mizel's top lieutenant. Perhaps more than anyone, he was responsible for M.D.C.'s meteoric performance in the early '80s. He negotiated land deals that dazzled his colleagues, who said he had a "brilliant head for land." He worked 90 hours a week and considered weekends as much a workday as any other. Like Mizel, Mandarich worked at a furious pace under the belief that opportunities came only to those who moved fast enough to catch them. "Everyone else should get out of the way because I'm going to run them down, and I have no use for them," he was reported to have said. It was a philosophy that he once credited to his military service as a light weapons infantryman in Vietnam.

Mandarich expected his employees to keep up with his pace. When they didn't, he sometimes flew into manic rages, screaming and swearing or hurling the 210 pounds of his 5-foot 9-inch frame in hysterical sprints through the sixth floor, which was his domain. He jumped on top of desks and threw telephones. A former executive tells a story about complaining to Mandarich once that deadlines were unrealistic, putting undo pressure on the staff. Mandarich's face blanched with rage. "You don't know what pressure is," he said, his voice low and trembling. "Try killing gooks for a living. Try getting shot at by gooks." He was shrieking now. "Goddamn it, I'll show you what fucking pressure is. Get the fuck out of my sight. Get the fuck out." The executive fled in terror and never complained again.

Despite his lack of finesse when it came to exchanges with his employees, he was invaluable to Mizel. He was the front-line man who played hardball, did the dirty work, slogged in the trenches while Mizel wheeled and dealed from his ninth-floor suite. Indeed, employees rarely, if ever, saw Mizel. Instead, the chairman's orders were relayed from the ninth floor via a speaker phone on Mandarich's desk.

It was for that purpose that the three men had gathered in Mandarich's office. Mandarich was behind his desk. His brother Gary Mandarich sat across from him. Mark Stenzel, a Richmond executive, sat next to Gary.

"David?" The voice on the speaker phone was that of Larry Mizel's secretary. "Larry wants $15,000 by five o'clock today. Can you take care of it."

It was an order, not a question, and Mandarich knew what she meant. Campaigns for Colorado governor were beginning to heat up —boil over, really—as contenders scrambled into position for the November election. Of the candidates, two were emerging as favorites, Republican Ted Strickland and Democrat Roy Romer. It was already a dirty fight. Each was running up expensive campaign bills and needed money. When a campaign—any campaign—ran short of cash, it came to Mizel. Nobody knew how he came up with the money, but he always did. Buckets of it. Campaign finance chairmen could put in a request hours before a deadline, and Mizel would have the money delivered. In political circles, it earned him the nickname "Magic Mizel."

Mandarich swung around in his chair and barked orders. "All right, Gary," he said to his brother, "you get $7,500, and you (pointing to Stenzel) get $7,500. Have it to me by four o'clock. Go."

Stenzel ran out of the office and down a flight of stairs. He knew what to do. It was a drill that recently had become a twice-weekly exercise, taking almost as much time as the job he was hired for—managing construction of residential developments. Nearing his office, he yelled across the room at two of his project managers. "We've got to get $7,500 by four o'clock. Drop what you're doing and get on the horn. We'll split it up." Stenzel got out a list of names and phone numbers and started dialing. On the list were plumbers, concrete workers, gravel companies, landscapers, drywallers, all of whom depended on M.D.C. for work. By mid 1986, M.D.C. was one of the only companies in Denver still putting up homes. Everyone else had withered under the weight of the fledgling recession, and subcontractors fought bitterly for jobs. If you had work, you did what it took to keep it. In M.D.C.'s eyes, it meant cutting a check for M.D.C.'s candidates when you were asked.

Stenzel and his project managers began working the phones. In most cases, they didn't need to spell out their threat. It was usually understood. Nonetheless, some of the subcontractors began to complain about the enormous sums of money they were doling out on M.D.C.'s behalf. Stenzel couldn't come up with the money, so he went back to Mandarich. "The subs are fed up," he said. "I just can't get the money. They're all tapped out."

Mandarich retorted: "You're landscaping some show homes right now, aren't you?"

"Yeah, I am."

"How much are the contracts for?"

"$9,000 a yard."

"Just raise the contracts to $16,000 a yard. You have the guys give you back $7,000 on each yard. There's $21,000."

It was the birth of a money-laundering scheme that would flower into a political money machine. Hundreds of thousands of dollars would come from M.D.C. through its subcontractors. The instructions were always explicit: Make out a personal check to the candidate and deliver it to M.D.C. headquarters. If there was a problem delivering the check, M.D.C. would be happy to send a cab to fetch it. Stenzel and his project managers rounded up the money, and M.D.C. delivered it to the candidate.

That day in 1986 was routine at M.D.C. Stenzel and scores of other M.D.C. employees in Arizona, California and Colorado systematically pressured subcontractors for at least three years, from 1985 to 1988. When the subcontractors wouldn't pay, they were threatened or reimbursed—sometimes both. M.D.C. delivered contributions to politicians all over the state and in Washington, often presenting them with a cover letter on M.D.C. letterhead.

The peculiar thing was that M.D.C. didn't pick its favorite candidates to supply with money; it gave to everyone. The company gave to Republicans and Democrats running for the same office. Curiously, Silverado and Bill Walters also were pumping extraordinary amounts of money into many of the same campaigns. By 1988, M.D.C., Silverado and Walters had donated nearly $1 million to candidates for governor, mayor, county commissioner and a spate of other local seats. Thousands more went to national campaigns for Congress and the presidency. No one, it seemed, was untouched.

When the M.D.C. contribution scheme came to light in the summer of 1990, it spurred investigations by the Federal Election Commission, the Internal Revenue Service, Colorado and federal grand juries, a special Colorado prosecutor and the Denver Election Commission. "I don't think anybody knows the depth of this thing," said former Colorado Attorney General Duane Woodard. "It goes everywhere: Democrats, Republicans, local, national. It's very broad and very deep." Woodard was removed from the investigation when it was discovered that his own campaign had received an M.D.C. donation.

Another investigator, overwhelmed by the seemingly never-ending reach of the case, moaned: "It's madness, absolute madness." But there may have been a method to the madness. M.D.C. needed influence. So did Silverado and Walters. They needed it because of a flurry of land transactions involving more than 7,000 acres of dusty grassland northeast of Denver that had begun a little less than two years earlier.

It was September 1985, shortly after Silverado had formed its real estate subsidiary, when Richard Schierburg and Steve Arent negotiated the purchase of thirty-nine acres of farmland in the plains north of Denver. It was one of their first acquisitions for Silverado-Elektra, but if they were trying to prove their acumen in the field, it didn't appear they had much of a future in real estate. For an absurdly high $38,000 an acre, Silverado bought itself a dry-wheat farm that its owners called The Little Buckaroo Ranch after the lullaby "Go to Sleep, My Little Buckaroo."

Walt and Wilma Horkans, who sold the ranch to Silverado before moving to upstate New York, had loved the place. They had horses and Colorado sunsets. But it just didn't seem like a savvy investment for Silverado. In terms of development, Little Buckaroo was smack in the middle of nowhere. For the better part of six years, money-making development had been in Southeast Denver, where people couldn't buy enough houses, rent enough office space or shop in enough malls. But here was nothing but dry prairie. The picture suddenly became very different four months later in the office of Denver Mayor Federico Pena.

It was January 28, 1985. Pena, brimming with pride, scanned the crowd of reporters and city dignitaries who packed his wood-paneled office on the second floor of the Denver City and County Building. Flanked by Adams County commissioners and a score of maps and real estate zoning charts, Pena stepped forward and quieted the crowd. A historic agreement had been reached, he said. Denver would build a new international airport. At a cost of $2 billion, it would be the largest public works project in the nation and become the busiest airport in the world. It would be as big as the Dallas-Fort Worth airport and bigger than Chicago's O'Hare and Hartsfield International in Atlanta. It was just the boost Denver's economy needed. With huge open spaces, futuristic sculptures and forty-foot escalators leading to underground trains where passengers would be directed by electronic voices, the airport would make Denver the hub of the Western United States, possibly the world, the mayor beamed. It would also make the land surrounding the project, in the words of Adams County Commission Chairman Steve Cramer, "the hottest development area in the country."

The mayor turned to one of the maps and with a pointer traced the outline of 15,000 acres of Adams County land where the airport would lie. The Little Buckaroo Ranch was squarely to the south of its anticipated southern border, near the proposed path of a main access road. At that moment, there probably was no better thirty-nine acres anywhere near the city. In the course of a twenty-minute press conference, Little Buckaroo, a seemingly worthless investment, was transformed to big bucks.

The next day, M.D.C. Holdings Inc. announced that it also had purchased land—877 acres known as the Upland Tract—adjacent to Little Buckaroo. It was M.D.C.'s largest land purchase, President Michael Feiner said at the time. "We think this is one of the most exciting pieces of ground in Denver." It was the understatement of the year. By acquiring the land before the airport was announced at 69 to 94 cents a square foot, for a total of $22.4 million, M.D.C. stood to make ten times that if an airport was put on the spot announced in the mayor's office.

The fact that Silverado and M.D.C. both bought such strategically placed property before the public knew about the airport poses the question of how they knew about it. Maybe they didn't. Maybe they took a gamble. Denver had been talking about a new airport for nearly a decade, and rumors had been circulating about the possibility of a site in Adams County. But until the January press conference, the prevailing wisdom (and the official position) had been that if there was to be new airport construction, it would be to expand the existing Stapleton International. Pena, who wanted a new airport, had initiated secret negotiations between Denver and Adams County over some thorny questions revolving around land annexation. For nearly a year, the two governments had bickered behind closed doors about the site and who would get tax revenues, who would service utilities and so forth. No one was supposed to have known about those negotiations until the agreement was announced that day in the mayor's office.

After the announcement, M.D.C., Silverado and Bill Walters went crazy buying land around the site. Walters bought 4,000 acres just north of the airport site on December 6, 1985. He paid for it with a $26 million loan from Silverado. Walters had so many Silverado loans at that point that if he couldn't make payments, the thrift's capital would be wiped out and Silverado would be insolvent. Nonetheless, Silverado made the loans without any guarantees from Walters or an appraisal on the land.

The buying spree continued with Silverado handing out most of the money. Walters bought the 1,200-acre Gun Club property south of the airport. Silverado paid him $8 million for a stake in the ownership. In another deal, Silverado gave Walters $3 million for a down payment on 2,689 acres near the proposed highway leading to the proposed airport. M.D.C. bought another 1,300 acres just south of the site. Altogether, Silverado, M.D.C. and Walters amassed more than 10,000 acres. In loans and real estate investments, Silverado had plowed more than $70 million of depositors' money into airport land.

No sooner did they have the property in their hands than they began buying and selling it among themselves, inflating the prices and making a killing each time land changed hands. In the summer of 1985, for instance, Silverado-Elektra sold Little Buckaroo to Wayne Gardenswartz. Gardenswartz was a strawbuyer, someone who buys land (usually with someone else's money), holds it for a while, then resells it to someone else. He was a former M.D.C. chief financial officer whose business address was the same as Mandarich's, and he appeared to operate at Mandarich's direction. Gardenswartz bought little Buckaroo at 150 percent of the price Silverado-Elektra had paid just ten months before.

Gardenswartz got most of the money to buy Little Buckaroo in a loan from Silverado Banking. That way, Silverado made money coming and going: Silverado-Elektra booked a profit from the land sale, and Silverado Banking booked a profit from the fees, at the same time putting a new performing loan on its books.

M.D.C. gave Gardenswartz the rest of the money he needed for the deal. Using $1.1 million that Silverado paid to M.D.C. in a separate transaction, the home builder bought a 75 percent share of any profits when the land sold again, which it did a little more than a year later. This time it was purchased by another strawbuyer, also apparently a puppet of M.D.C. LBR Enterprises Inc., owned and run by another former M.D.C. executive, bought Little Buckaroo from Gardenswartz for $4.29 million, allowing M.D.C. to book profits. Once again, Silverado made the loan, allowing it to book loan fees.

It wasn't an isolated case. Thousands of acres of airport land moved in similar ways between Silverado and Walters, Walters and M.D.C., M.D.C. and Silverado. Each time, they all made money, and Silverado was the piggy bank. It was a perfect scam. Everyone prospered as long as the clique held together.

And the clique would hold together for the simple reason that each party would be in serious financial trouble if it didn't. The airport deals connected Walters, Silverado and

M.D.C. like rock climbers attached by a rope. If one of them slipped, they all got hurt together. If Walters defaulted on his loans from Silverado, the thrift's capital position would be nearly wiped out. If Silverado went down, M.D.C. and Walters would lose millions on the Silverado stock they owned. These were millions neither could afford to lose in the slipping real estate market.

What's more, by inflating prices on land by trading it among themselves, they were stacking more and more chips on one bet. The more they inflated land prices artificially, the more they stood to lose if the airport didn't come through.

But the airport was a done deal, right? Wrong. It faced a long, fierce battle in Congress, Colorado state government, Denver city government and Adams County government. All would be beneficiaries of M.D.C.'s political fund-raising machine, whose tachometer hit red in 1986 as candidates hurled mud at one another in the race for Colorado governor.

Whoever took office as the state's chief executive was seen as a key to resolving the bickering that had erupted again between Adams County and Denver over the airport's location. Checks from M.D.C. contractors flooded war chests. So did money from M.D.C. itself and from Silverado and Walters, helping to make the race the most expensive campaign in Colorado history. The contributions focused first on Republican Ted Strickland, who held an early lead, then shifted to Democrat Roy Romer, with most of the money rushing in during the last two months of the campaign, when Romer's lead appeared immutable. Romer won, and in his first speech after being elected November 4, he vowed to "make sure the airport happens." In the weeks that followed, Silverado, Walters and M.D.C. continued to put money into Romer's camp. The contributions made up nearly $100,000 of his total $1.8 million war chest.

Soon after Romer was elected, the airport deal looked as though it might fall apart, and a groundswell of support for alternative sites appeared. Romer stood stalwartly by the original site, a position that his political foes said was a result of the heavy contributions. Romer later appointed Mizel to the Colorado Economic Development Council, where Mizel wanted to use the council's $1.4 million budget to support the airport.

The same year that contributions began to flow heavily, Mizel, Walters and Wise all assumed influential positions in Denver's business community, ultimately playing key roles in lobbying for the airport and its location. Wise became treasurer of the Greater Denver Chamber of Commerce, which was to hand over huge sums of money to airport-related campaigns, and Walters became chairman of the group. Mizel, meanwhile, chaired Colorado Concern, which became known as the state's "super PAC" for its lavish giving. That year, it handed out $86,000 to Colorado legislators. The following spring, the legislature passed a bill allowing the state to take control of the airport approval process if Denver's negotiations fell through.

Still, the airport was on precarious ground as campaigns for the 1987 Denver mayoral elections started up. By that time Mizel, Silverado and Walters were considered the wellspring of political money. To ignore it was political suicide. "Everybody knew that you had to get in with those guys before you could get anywhere in this town," said an official for Pena's re-election campaign. "You had to access that core group of money people or your political boat was sunk."

The stakes in the mayoral elections were high. The Denver mayor would perhaps be the single most influential politician in securing the project. The Mizel machine went to work first on Michael Licht, a city auditor making a run at incumbent Pena.

Licht immediately won unexpected support, running an unrelenting campaign against the new airport. There was no proof Denver needed it, he said, and enough people agreed for him to show favorably in the polls.

But disaster struck his campaign in February, just three months before the election. Newspaper reports alleged that he had forced staff in his city auditor's office to help run his mayoral campaign, and the Denver Election Commission hopped on his back. The campaign began to self-destruct.

The bad publicity wrecked his image and, worse, donations virtually stopped—until Magic Mizel paid him a visit.

"The campaign at that point was pretty well down the tubes," Licht said in a 1990 interview. "Larry indicated to me that he could help me out, and that was the extent of the conversation. We were right in the middle of the campaign. He said he thought he knew some folks who might want to help out." Licht abruptly became a staunch airport supporter, and weeks later, $80,000 from M.D.C. contractors in Colorado, Arizona and California dumped into Licht's war chest. Explaining his switch on the airport in 1990, Licht said, "You have to be flexible."

Even with the money from M.D.C. subcontractors, it soon was clear that Licht wouldn't win the May 19 primary. Instead, Pena and Denver lawyer Donald Bain advanced to a June runoff, and support from M.D.C. subcontractors along with Silverado and Walters shifted to those candidates. Bain held the early lead, and that's where the money focused. But when Pena began to pull ahead, the dollars moved. The two campaigns fought one another and battled for funding. "We were substantially behind, and we didn't have any money," said the former Pena campaign official. "There were four weeks to go in the campaign. At that point you don't ask questions. They were outspending us and they were ahead in the polls. We had to get a lot of money fast. The way it usually works is that you go to someone who's been good to you in the past and see what they can do for you. The thing is that those people get a lot of access to the candidate. It's usually pretty subtle. They would say, 'Boy, you could really help us out on something.' You'd be hard pressed not to be a little accommodating."

Mizel won audiences with the new mayor, who wanted the airport as much as Mizel did. Pena never reversed his position on a new airport the way Licht did. Indeed, Pena saw the project as a crowning achievement of his administration. But in the summer of 1987, shortly after Pena was elected, the project still faced considerable political opposition, and the mayor had to play his cards carefully. Mizel became the voice that whispered in Pena's ear about the desires of the business community. As the man who had given more than virtually anyone else, he was the voice of the private sector. "The fact is that (Mizel) supported the airport," Pena said in a 1990 interview. "He wanted it built and so did I. My goals were synonymous with Larry's goals and with the goals of the business community."

In August, Pena halted improvement work at the existing Stapleton International, one of the last outward signs that a new airport wouldn't fly. Stopping the work meant Pena was committed, and Mizel, Walters and Silverado redirected their efforts to pouring gravy on the feast.

As any real estate developer worth his salt knows, an airport crams a big building full of people who wouldn't have any place to go if there weren't highways. Along those highways, people buy gas, stop at convenience stores and look for a place to stay for the night. Highways mean money to real estate developers who have land along them. Bill Walters happened to have some. Planners envisioned a beltway circling the northeast edge of the city and leading to the airport, passing through or near two Walters parcels, one of which was financed by Silverado. Walters had donated office space to the E-470 Authority, which was responsible for planning and building the highway.

The project foundered on budget problems in fall 1987, and a group of concerned businessmen—including Mizel and Walters—met to see what they could do about it. Mizel suggested they convince the Colorado Legislature to approve a bond issue to pay for the deal. State Democrats would never go for it, one of the businessmen worried. "Forget about them Dems," Mizel reportedly snapped. "We can buy them."

The airport, meanwhile, was caught up once again in a fight between Adams County and Denver. Again, it was on the brink of disaster. No one seemed able to resolve the dispute, so Adams County voters were asked to settle the issue on a special ballot scheduled for May 1988. Adams County apparently thought it was on the losing end of a pretty big deal in which Denver would get the benefits of an airport and the county would get the noise and pollution. A massive public relations campaign was launched, funded almost entirely by donations from M.D.C., Silverado, Walters and the Greater Denver Corp., an arm of the Greater Denver Chamber of Commerce, where Walters was chairman and Wise was treasurer.

Wise whipped his employees into a pro-airport frenzy. Silverado's go-go bankers carried signs, mounted telephone campaigns to encourage voters and volunteered to drive people to the polls. "I've never seen anything like it," one executive said. "For a long time, that's all people talked about around the office, the airport and the E-470 project."

In May 1988, Adams County voters approved the airport. But it was too late to save Silverado. A team of twenty regulators from the Federal Home Loan Bank of Topeka, Kansas, had worked nearly around the clock since December 1, 1986, to unravel transactions that had disguised more than $200 million in Silverado losses.

Part III

Checks and Balances

8

Toothless Tiger

Topeka, Kansas, is a weary, battered-looking town, as though a hundred years of wind and prairie dust had parched the life from its buildings and streets. Even the relatively new office towers of its modest downtown look haggard, their luster scoured away by the emptiness of the central Kansas plains. The Depression-era fathers of the savings and loan industry believed that cities like Topeka—middle-American cities, where middle- class Americans worked and bought homes and died—represented the ideals of the industry, so that's where they put some of the twelve regional Federal Home Loan Banks to fund and regulate thrifts. The banks were set up with two roles. One was to lend money to thrifts in their respective districts, helping them through bad times. The other was to regulate.

Regulators are trained like soldiers or cops. Their job, so the training goes, is to protect the deposit insurance fund from thrift failures. In the parlance of the industry, they are the second line of defense—after boards of directors—to protect taxpayers from bad apples who might rot the barrel.

In many ways, the regulator has a thankless job. In the Reagan years, pay was lean and staffs too small. Good regulators often need degrees in accounting or law, which in the private sector could draw twice and triple a starting regulator's salary. In the 1980s, that often meant the Home Loan Banks hired CPAs and lawyers who weren't good enough to do anything else. But there were exceptions— people who were good at what they did and for one reason or another found their calling in towns like Topeka. One of them was Dorothy van Cleave.

It was November, 1986. The light in van Cleave's office was the only one burning in the Topeka bank headquarters as she prepared for what would become the largest examination ever assembled for a single thrift, requiring a team of twenty examiners and an incredible 7,000 hours to unravel the intricate fibers of Silverado's operation. She was poring over the Silverado documents that in less than three months would lead examiners to conclude that the savings and loan was out of control and dangerously close to insolvency. By January, 1987, six months before the examination was completed, van Cleave would know enough to see that Silverado was in grave danger of failing. The months leading to the examination and the attempts to bring Silverado under control were an odyssey in bungled bureaucracy, incompetency and self-interest at the Topeka headquarters.

Van Cleave was one of the best examiners the Topeka bank had. An accountant by training, she looked the part— sedate, stoic. Like the rest of the supervisory examiners at the Topeka bank, she had a small government-issue cubicle in a long row of identical offices, divided like stables along one wall of the second floor. Cardboard boxes crammed with financial documents littered her office, on the floor, a bookshelf, and two chairs meant for visitors. The bare walls, painted government beige, lent it a monastic air, and van Cleave worked with a silent, monk-like devotion. Often, she was the first to arrive each morning and the last to leave, tucking papers into a battered maroon briefcase. On a shelf behind her desk, placed in such a way as to suggest reverence, was an aging, well-thumbed copy of a 1969 government report, "Study of the Savings and Loan Industry," her scripture.

As the examiner in charge of Silverado, it was van Cleave's job to sift through the institution's documents and report her findings to her superiors. She had been unceremoniously handed the assignment three months earlier in September the way that all assignments are handed out at the Topeka bank: with a memo. Examination responsibilities were routinely shifted among examiners, partly to distribute workloads and partly to maintain objectivity in the examination process. Van Cleave's field manager had posted new assignments with her name slotted by the Denver thrift. Boxes of Silverado's papers and past exams were wheeled into her office, and she set about the task of what regulators call scoping.

Scoping is nothing more than reviewing an institution, bringing oneself up to speed like a doctor reviewing the medical records of a new patient. In most cases, scoping takes days, weeks for more complex thrifts. Silverado required more than a month. It was the longest, most excruciating study of her career. Working nights and weekends, drinking coffee to stay awake, she plowed through the documents, trying to wrap her hands around Silverado's transactions, which always seemed to disappear, like smoke. She would later say simply: "It was hell."

About the same time van Cleave got her assignment, another regulator—Terry Sandefur—was also put on the case. Sandefur was an analyst, one step above van Cleave in the supervisory hierarchy. Analysts review the reports assembled by the examiners and make recommendations about what action, if any, regulators should take. Like van Cleave, Sandefur had picked through the mind-numbing array of numbers and had begun to piece together the puzzle. They found $10 million in loan losses Silverado had simply covered up. But despite the unrecognized losses, the thrift didn't seem to be in terribly poor condition. Its capital level was well above regulatory standards. But as they waded deeper into the maze, they found the mirrors Silverado had used to disguise its condition, and when they wheeled them away they found mountains of worthless paper and capital that existed only on the books. Silverado was in deep trouble.

There was something disturbing about their findings that had less to do with Silverado than with the Topeka bank itself. Silverado had been on the edge for years, and its nefarious dealings had been in plain sight, just as they were now. Why hadn't anyone caught them before? Maybe none of the regulators had been as good as van Cleave and Sandefur. Or perhaps their overworked predecessors had simply missed them. After all, examiners were carrying unbelievable workloads in the wake of Reagan budget cuts, which had lopped hundreds of federal thrift examiners off the payroll. Sandefur alone was dealing with thirty troubled thrifts at once. Mistakes could be explained. But mistakes didn't explain why the Topeka bank had actually approved most of Silverado's illegal and wildly imprudent transactions.

The man in charge of those approvals was Kermit Mowbray, president of the Topeka bank. Mowbray was a timid, nervous- looking man who had come up through the bank as an economist. He liked the abstraction of his science, which is perhaps why he didn't get on well with people. That's not to say he wasn't personable. He was. But when situations got heated or when events threatened to spin out of control, he seemed to cower. He stammered and squeezed his eyes shut, comically shifting his hedge-like eyebrows up and down. Mowbray's great weakness was that he liked to be liked. He sought approval and reassurance from the people around him, including the executives of the savings and loans in his district. "He struck me as a guy who, well, he ran the smallest bank in the system," said Ed Gray, who, as chairman of the Federal Home Loan Bank Board in Washington, was Mowbray's boss. "Let's not kid ourselves: Topeka isn't like San Francisco or one of the other big-city banks. He was the small time trying to be big-time. He always seemed to me to be someone who wanted to play the game, be one of the boys, but he couldn't quite make it. He wanted to go to every trade meeting in sight because that's where he could pal around with his buddies."

Gray considered the weakness such a problem that he contemplated firing Mowbray in the mid 1980s. "I was concerned about the apparent, if not the actual, conflicts of interest that were at work," he said. "He was the weakest link in the chain, and I didn't think he could stand up to the pressures that seemed to be there at the time." In the end, Gray didn't fire Mowbray because Gray was already in trouble with the Home Loan Bank presidents for firing the president of the Dallas bank. "It was all for one, one for all with those guys," Gray said. "Getting rid of Mowbray would have been like throwing a gasoline bomb in their midst."

In a way, Mowbray might be forgiven. The Home Loan Bank system was set up both as regulator and advocate. At the same time they were supervising thrifts, the banks were meant to promote the industry. Generally, the regulatory staffs were kept separate from the portions of the bank geared to supporting thrifts. But splitting the president wasn't possible; he was expected to be both top cop and best friend. It was a ridiculous setup, prone to conflicts of interest if not emotional confusion.

To Michael Wise, Mowbray's need was like the soft underbelly of a fattened prey, and he exploited it mercilessly. From the moment Wise took Silverado's helm, he cultivated his acquaintance with Mowbray into a friendship. Indeed, it was Mowbray who recommended that Mile High hire Wise in the first place. The two sat in Mowbray's office for long stretches, the sound of laughter coming through the closed door. Wise wrote Mowbray personal notes from time to time and flew regularly to Topeka. Mowbray often sent a driver to pick Wise up in his Lincoln, sparing Wise the hassle and expense of the hour-long taxi ride from Kansas City International Airport. On one occasion, when Wise called unexpectedly from the airport, Mowbray snubbed another Denver savings and loan executive who had come to Topeka to discuss a problem at his thrift. "I waited for four hours in that waiting room, and he wouldn't see me," the executive said.

"I had an appointment, and he blew me off for this guy who just blew into town."

In 1981, Wise became a director of the Topeka bank's board, over which Mowbray presided. The board was another peculiar arrangement in the regulatory system. For the most part, the board was composed of thrift executives, who helped set the direction of the bank. In effect, it was thrift executives regulating the regulators. It also helped thrift executives pressure regulators into going soft on exams. The savings and loans in each district actually owned a portion of home loan bank, in the form of stock they were required to purchase. That meant a director could come down on the president when the regulatory heat was turned up just by saying: "We own you."

Wise was never so blunt. He had a way of looking disappointed in Mowbray when the bank president didn't understand one of Silverado's proposals. And Wise dazzled him with slide shows and flip charts in the board room next to Mowbray's office. "He came in and gave these presentations about things they were doing," Mowbray said in 1990. "He presented a polished figure. He had the aura of being unflappable, like he knew exactly what he was doing."

And so Mowbray signed off on deal after deal that his own regulators would later say were illegal, or at best, wildly imprudent. Indeed, he became a true believer in Silverado's ways and one of the thrift's fiercest defenders. He once exploded in rage over lunch at a Denver hotel when a retired savings and loan executive suggested that Silverado was in trouble. "If any thrift in this state is in trouble, it's not Silverado," Mowbray reportedly said, stammering, his face crimson. "That thrift is run by—we—it's the best damn management I've ever seen."

Van Cleave and Sandefur had other things to worry about, however. Based on the documents they had scrutinized since September, they had plotted strategy for a full-fledged exam to begin December 1, 1986. They believed Silverado was in bad shape, but they apparently didn't have any idea of the task on which they were about to embark.

They began the examination with a standard team of four field examiners. But after a month digging through records in Silverado's internal auditing department, they had only scratched the surface. The more they dug, the more skeletons they found, and they sent for help. This time, van Cleave pulled out the stops, taking examiners off other assignments in Oklahoma City, Wichita and Lincoln, Nebraska. In all, she marshalled twenty examiners and mounted her attack. She divided her forces into teams and stationed them on the first, second, twelfth and thirteenth floors of Silverado Center One. One team examined Silverado's loan papers, another combed the thrift's financial statements, another dissected the workings of Silverado-Elektra and other subsidiaries and a fourth examined management. Some 40,000 pages of documents were hauled to two adjoining conference rooms on the twelfth floor. Van Cleave managed the show from the penthouse suite.

They worked around the clock, catching catnaps at the hotel across the street. But by mid-January, already haggard from the sheer volume of work, they were no nearer to being done. They had, however, found enough to know that Silverado's financial position—disguised as it was—was sinking like a rock. Each team had unearthed a litany of illegal transactions and cases in which Wise and Lewis had simply lied to regulators. They found the year-end 1986 deals. They found the land swaps with M.D.C. They found the Walters loans. The Good loans. Still, it was getting deeper.

The situation was critical. Regulators couldn't wait to complete the exam, which could take months longer, before taking some kind of action. So van Cleave typed up the examiners' findings and sent them back to Sandefur in Topeka. Sandefur called the Home Loan Bank's enforcement division in Washington and turned the reports over to the Topeka bank's lawyer. There was no question: The thrift was hemorrhaging, and it had to be stopped.

They decided upon a cease-and-desist order, the most powerful weapon in the regulatory arsenal short of seizure. The order in effect would put the thrift under tight government control. Silverado would be forced to stop the quid pro quo deals and to answer to regulators before embarking on new ventures. Regulators could enforce the action, if necessary, in federal court. But the management of the thrift would have to agree to the order. In other words, regulators would have to build a water-tight case, then strong-arm management into accepting it, like cops squeezing a confession out of a suspect. Van Cleave thought they had a case. So did Sandefur and so did Washington. On March 9, they flew to Denver, where they would confront Silverado management the next day.

March 10 dawned with a cold, hard sky whose darkness pressed against the windows of the Skydeck as the confrontation began at 9 a.m. in the board room. Regulators sat across the long conference table from Silverado's board and executives. Wise sat silently at one end, his hands folded on the table. After a brief introduction, Sandefur began methodically pounding one nail after another into the coffin. He detailed the examiners' findings, paused to listen to protests from Wise and Lewis, then moved to the next subject. So the meeting went for two hours, the regulators hammering each point as they tried to move toward their goal.

At 11 a.m., the group took a break, and Kermit Mowbray's right-hand man, Tommie Thompson, slipped from the room and found a telephone. He dialed, talked quietly for a few moments, hung up and returned to the meeting. He had an astonishing announcement: "Mowbray says drop the C&D."

The regulators were stunned. Their case had just taken a baseball bat to the solar plexus, and their own boss had done the swinging. Without the authority to issue a cease-and-desist order, they were powerless. Mowbray later defended his move by saying he wanted to be absolutely sure before taking action. But a memo written by Silverado's public accountants tells a more revealing story. When Wise learned the examiners were planning the March 10 confrontation, he telephoned Mowbray in Topeka, the memo says. Wise asked him what the meeting was about, and Mowbray said he didn't know of any meeting but he'd check on it. He did and called Wise back. A cease-and-desist order, he assured Wise, was out of the question. Mowbray later denied the conversation took place.

Sandefur, van Cleave, two other regulators and Mc-Cormally, the Topeka bank's lawyer, retreated to a corner of the room and huddled for ten minutes, talking in whispers. McCormally was incensed. They weren't going to walk out of Silverado without stopping the quid pro quo and real estate-for-stock deals, he said. The others agreed, but they no longer had authority to force Silverado to do anything. Their only option was a supervisory directive, an instruction the institution could disregard if it felt so inclined.

Still, it was all they had. So Sandefur went back to the table, and with as much authority as he could muster, he ordered the thrift to stop the loan-for-stock deals, the loan-pool deals, the quid pro quo deals. They were paper threats, but it was all they could do. Then they went home. Vandapool later bragged to Silverado's public accountants that he and the other Silverado executives had run the regulators out of town. He added that Sandefur got his hand slapped and was replaced on the Silverado case and van Cleave was demoted to a clerical job. None of it was true, of course.

Silverado ignored the directive and continued as it had before. It continued to sell participations in the loan pool, continued trading real estate for stock and continued lending cash for trash.

On March 27, the thrift committed an act of utter insanity. It lent $74 million to a Texas developer for 330 acres of barren property in Fort Worth. Every aspect of the deal looked bad. At the time, the Texas real estate market was possibly the worst in the nation, and property values were plunging almost daily. Worse, the loan was for undeveloped land, the riskiest kind of collateral. Worse still, it was secured by second liens on the property, meaning that in the event of a default, the first lienholder would get $41 million from the property before Silverado saw a dime. Silverado also agreed that if the developer defaulted on the first lien, Silverado would pick up the $30 million tab. Silverado had left itself open to $100 million of risk on a deal that couldn't possibly hold together. It simply didn't make sense. Oh, but it did.

Silverado probably never intended for the loan to be a wise investment. It desperately needed someone to take huge blocks of bad loans off its books and to pump capital into the company. All the cash-for-trash and quid pro quo deals, while making Silverado look good, worked like a powerfully addictive narcotic. Every time the thrift got a fix, it felt great for a while. But then developers stopped paying on the dangerous loans it had made, and it needed another fix. In March 1987, Silverado was like a junky strung out in an alley. It was coming down hard and fast, and it was willing to pay anything for its next fix. The Fort Worth loan was the dope it was looking for.

Of the $74 million Silverado lent on the deal, only $10.5 million went to developing the property. The developer used $17.8 million to buy bad loans from the loan pool and pocketed another $22 million. Silverado tucked away the rest in a special account to make payments on the loan so that it would look like a healthy asset even though the developer didn't make payments. At the March board meeting, when the deal was presented, Richard Bunchman voted against it. He told Congress in 1990 that his conscience wouldn't let him approve it. It was the first time in nearly a decade that a Silverado director had dissented.

Wise began to recede from the reality of Silverado's troubles. He spent more and more time in the Skydeck, locked in his office. "At that point, you never saw Mike around the office," an executive vice president said. "He never came down from on high. There was something eerie about the whole thing. There were times when I had to go up there, and it was deathly quiet. My heals clicked on the floor because they were marble, and the sound echoed everywhere. But Mike didn't make any noise. It was like he drifted—he just appeared. He was a mystery man —I can't explain it—a mystique."

Wise became obsessed with his safety. Suddenly and inexplicably, he ordered an elaborate security system. He had daily escorts by armed guards to and from his navy blue Mercedes, which stayed under the surveillance of an electronic eye in Silverado's garage. More armed guards patrolled each floor of the tower. A phalanx of guards was reserved for the Skydeck.

A secret concrete bunker, equipped with phone, desk and small refrigerator, was installed adjacent to Wise's office. Once inside, Wise could lock the door with a two-inch steel dead bolt and gaze out into his office through a peephole in the door. And as Wise drifted from reality, so did his employees. "After a while, it was like nothing was real at Silverado anymore. People got really wound up in this fantasy they had. It was like we were totally detached from reality," an executive vice president recalled.

Wise worked in silence for hours on end behind the closed door of his office, plotting the ultimate expansion of Silverado into a nationwide company. Despite the tightening regulatory noose, Wise believed Silverado could outsmart— or outrun—its opponents, and he wanted Silverado's name carried across the land. "Mike wanted to take Silverado nationwide," said an executive who was close to Wise. "That was his dream. He wanted to buy Beverly Hills (Savings and Loan), he wanted to be able to do business anywhere in the country."

At an April meeting, Wise had presented Mowbray a letter detailing a plan to begin his nationwide plunge by acquiring a thrift in Topeka with the right to branch into four states. Sandefur, who attended the meeting, was incredulous. But the proposal didn't faze Mowbray. Sandefur later assured him that Silverado was in no condition to be expanding, and the request was denied.

Back in Topeka, Mowbray moved into a new office in an executive suite he had helped design and decorate. He was immensely proud of the new arrangement. The oak parquet floors and mahogany- paneled walls were elegant. Two doors opened onto a kitchenette with a sink and a place where he could fix tea, and a big window made the office a bright, happy-looking place.

The reception area, just outside his office, was equally comfortable. With his secretary, Mowbray had helped pick out delicate Queen Anne furnishings, an imported Iranian rug and other accessories to give his domain an appropriately dignified air. It was an escape from the turmoil that surrounded Silverado and the conflicts that were beginning to rise between Mowbray and his regulators, such as the question of real estate appraisals.

Van Cleave had reburied herself in the examination. Regulators were powerless to do anything about the Fort Worth loan since Mowbray put a stop to the cease-and-desist order. So van Cleave devoted herself to other matters. By late spring, her loan team had dug up eighteen loans for which appraisals of the real estate collateralizing the loans looked grossly inflated, ostensibly so Silverado could lend extra money to developers who then bought Silverado stock and bad loans. She asked Silverado to correct the appraisals, but management refused. It was crucial to her examination to find out how much the real estate that collateralized Silverado's loans was really worth. If it was worth less than Silverado said it was, as she suspected, it meant the institution was covering up potentially huge losses.

The Topeka bank could do its own test appraisals to settle the matter, but appraisals cost money and Mowbray had to approve the expenditure. A meeting was arranged.

Sandefur, Thompson and McCormally met Mowbray in his office. McCormally spoke first. Examiners in the field would be paralyzed without appraisals to pin down Silverado's losses, he said. Mowbray fidgeted, perhaps because McCormally unnerved him. McCormally was one of the Topeka bank's rising stars. A tireless workhorse and a tough negotiator, he had earned more than one badge of honor for putting out fires in Oklahoma, where thrifts had dropped like flies in the early years of the S&L crisis. As boyish and Midwestern as McCormally looked, he could appear remarkably imposing just by setting his face in a blank stare, an eyebrow cocked just enough to suggest skepticism. He said only what he had to, letting his opponents babble their way into trouble.

Mowbray argued. He didn't think appraisals were necessary. McCormally argued back. Finally, his voice rising, Mowbray burst out: "The Federal Home Loan Bank is not going to appraise institutions out of business." McCormally was silent. "The adverse conditions in Colorado are short-term," he said. "Asset values will recover." The meeting ended.

It was June then. Mowbray stuck to his position until August, a month after van Cleave finished the Silverado examination. It required three hundred pages to list regulatory violations, illegal transactions, conflicts of interest, self-dealing, excessive compensation, poor documentation on loans, loans on preferential terms to officers and directors, distorted and inaccurate financial reporting, hidden problem loans. At least 26 percent of Silverado's loans were bad, and she had uncovered $43 million in unreported losses, even without new appraisals. The exam showed that Silverado didn't meet minimum capital requirements, despite the fact that Silverado said it had sufficient capital. Mowbray finally relented and allowed van Cleave to get new appraisals on ten of the questioned loans.

At the end of October, eight months after the regulators had tried to win a cease-and-desist order, Silverado's board agreed to a supervisory agreement, a lesser action. Under the terms of the agreement, Silverado was to abandon commercial real estate for home mortgage lending. Wise and Metz were ordered to repay the $4.5 million in loans Silverado had given them. The sweet terms on home loans Silverado had given to officers and directors, including Neil Bush, were to be revised. The excessive salaries to executives were to be brought in line.

It was a victory, but a small one. For Silverado's condition was growing rapidly worse, and the regulators were finding fault not only with the thrift but with its accounting firm, Coopers & Lybrand.

9

Don't Let the Pig Out

At the Denver offices of Coopers & Lybrand, a collection of exhausted, disheveled accountants stood in a conference room on the thirty-fourth floor of the Republic Plaza building. The long table that ran the length of the room was covered with stacks of Silverado's financial records. Hundreds of loose-leaf notebooks and bound reports lay in piles and boxes all over the room. Stacks that didn't fit on the table tilted precariously on chairs and on the floor. Some of the accountants ruffled tensely through the documents, checking figures. Taped to the door was a picture of a pig, gazing triumphantly into the room.

It was summer of 1988. There was fear in the room. Federal regulators were closing in on Silverado, and at the same time they were closing in on Coopers & Lybrand. It had become increasingly clear that the accounting firm had made terrible mistakes. Among other things, it had affirmed that Silverado had made a record $15 million profit in 1986 when it should have posted a $15 million loss. The firm had let Silverado executives take bonuses based on phantom earnings that year and had ignored signs that Silverado was near insolvency, reporting instead that it was in excellent financial health. Sandefur and McCormally from the Federal Home Loan

Bank of Topeka had already paid more than one visit to the firm.

The auditors smelled of coffee and sweat. Most of them had spent the past several months sifting through the paper blizzard twelve hours at a time, checking and rechecking to make sure they had done their job right. Some of them had hardly left the office, stepping out only to bathe with a few handfuls of tap water and a swipe with a deodorant stick.

One of the auditors broke the silence. "Fucking pig," he said, flipping a finger at the picture on the door. Any accountant could explain what he meant. A pig is a powerful and feared beast in the trade that symbolizes an audit out of control, paralyzed by confusion. He represents everything that can go wrong in an audit: Mistakes, errors in judgment and, worse, deliberate pandering to the client. Regulators would later conclude that Coopers & Lybrand had done those things in its audit of Silverado. If the accountants had been the financial sentinels they were supposed to be, Silverado might have been closed earlier, sparing taxpayers hundreds of millions of dollars. But for the time being, no one had drawn any conclusions. The pig was still in his pen.

A soft knock came at the door, and a senior accountant let himself in. He spoke for a moment in whispers to the auditor in charge and then left, letting the door swing open behind him. One of the accountants looked up from her work. "Hey, close the door," she barked, surprising herself with her own ferocity. "Don't let the pig out."

What had happened in that conference room over the two years Coopers & Lybrand had presided over Silverado's financial statements was the result of a firm in chaos. It had forgotten ethics and every other principle of the accounting profession in its blind pursuit of money. To understand how it happened, we must go back a few years to 1984, the year that Coopers & Lybrand's top brass decided its Denver office needed a swift kick. Denver had been one of the hottest growth areas in the country for accounting firms, but Coopers didn't perform up to snuff in the eyes of the home office in New York. So it sent in a man who had proved he was cut from the right cloth, a man who knew how to make a profit.

That man was Jack Grace. Grace believed in money. Giving it motivated people. Threatening to take it away motivated them even more. And making money for the company meant his own corporate success. These were his guiding principles, and his principles were what made him a fast climber in Coopers & Lybrand's rapidly expanding corporate ranks.

Like a number of other Big Eight accounting firms, Coopers & Lybrand was riding the crest of unprecedented business growth in the 1980s. The firm was prosperous and growing quickly. But it needed managers like Jack Grace who could crack the whip to keep profits rolling in as it grew. Grace had cut his teeth in a startup office in Albany, New York. He had worked such wonders there that the New York partners gave him a shot at Denver. "He was considered by the home office to be sort of a miracle boy with the numbers, and they wanted him out here," recalled a managing auditor in Denver. "The numbers here weren't what New York wanted, so they sent him out to see what he could do. We were doing fine before he came. We weren't making a lot of money, but it was respectable. I think we had a good reputation in the community, and there was a feeling among most of the people there that we were doing a good job. People were well trained, and I think we had an image of being tough but fair auditors." That changed in short order, however. "After Jack came, suddenly the bottom line was golden," the auditor said. "We all became prostitutes. Everything was for money."

Grace was not the sort of corporate leader who lost any sleep if his employees didn't like him. Respect was enough. He rarely smiled, traversing the gray-carpeted halls of Coopers & Lybrand's Denver office in what seemed a loosely controlled rage. His face was perpetually red, an uncomfortable red as though he had a horrible sunburn, highlighted by a shock of thick gray wire for hair. "He was one of those guys," an accountant said, "whose collar always seemed too tight. It was like there was all this pressure building up in there and one day his brains were going to blow out the top of his head." Another accountant said Grace reminded him of the tyrant Mr. Dithers in the comic strip "Blondie." Grace stormed about the office, a huge cigar wedged between his tightly clenched jaws. On bad days, he said nothing when greeted by other partners in the hallway. On good days, he grunted. He was a man to be feared.

Shortly after arriving in Denver, Grace called a meeting of the firm's managers. He slowly paced the meeting room, gnawing contemplatively on his cigar, which he had chewed to a soggy nub. He stopped near the front of the room, fists jammed into his pockets. He stared at the floor before leveling his gaze upon the expectant listeners. Twenty pairs of eyes riveted on him, not because he was an inspiring sight but because he was a fearful one. Grace pulled the nub of a cigar from his mouth and regarded it. Directing his words to the wad of tobacco in his hand, he spoke in a quiet monotone: "The numbers aren't good enough. Get them up. You can do it one of two ways: Jack up the fees or bring down the hours you spend on an audit. End of discussion." He put the remains of the cigar back in his mouth and left the room to silence from twenty blue suits. So this was the miracle man.

The managers filed out and went back to work, relieved for the most part that the encounter was over. But it wasn't, not really. The meeting was a watershed in the Coopers & Lybrand way of life in the Denver office. The idea that accountants hold a solemn duty to their profession, that objectivity must reign over all other things, was chipped away in scores of weekly meetings Grace held with his managers over the next several years. Grace paraded before them, berating them for not making enough money. "All we talked about was money. Dollars, dollars, dollars. Bottom line. That was it," one of the managers said. Grace encouraged the managers to charge more or spend less time on their audits, but "everybody knew that it was far too competitive out there to jack up the fees. Accounts would drop like flies," recalled one accountant, who quit the firm in disgust. "We didn't have a choice. That's when the real problems started. When you don't spend enough time on an audit, something's going to get missed. That's all there is to it."

Grace's pecuniary themes didn't start or end with the managers. Managers run audits. They allocate tasks to the working stiffs in the trenches and set the tone for how things get done. But the butter for the bread comes from the partners. Partners bring in business. Without them, no one else would have a job. In general, partners have big expense accounts and log a lot of time at parties and the golf course, on the off chance a prospective client might be there, too. They wine and dine Joe Blow CEO and rattle off facts and figures about his business. If they're lucky, Mr. Blow decides to give the firm his account. Sometimes, the best partners are the worst accountants, but they have some of the salesman's magic and reel in new accounts like nobody's business. Grace apparently didn't see enough of that quality in his partners when he arrived in 1984. So he started something called the Partner Review Program.

As a rule, the words "review program" strike fear in the hearts of any corporate employee. They ring with a wicked meaning: You'd better watch your ass or it's going to get chewed off. This was no exception. The Partner Review Program consisted essentially of monthly or quarterly meetings of the dozen or so Coopers & Lybrand partners in the Denver office. At each review meeting, Grace methodically reviewed the business each partner had brought in for the month or quarter. If he deemed it inadequate, he yelled and screamed and threatened. Coopers & Lybrand needed more accounts, damn it, and the partners were to see to it.

There's a certain logic to the program. It stands to reason that if a firm isn't getting enough business, the partner in charge should send his or her troops to get more. Unhappily, that wasn't the way it worked. Competition for accounts was already fierce in Denver. There simply weren't many free accounts floating around town. This posed a problem for the partners: how to bring in big money fast when there wasn't much work to be had. The answer, as it turned out, was to find clients unhappy with their present accounting firm and lure them into Coopers & Lybrand's open arms. If they were willing to pay a lot of money, so much the better. The problem, however, is that clients unhappy with their present auditors often are disgruntled with the tough scrutiny that they're receiving. And if they're willing to pay a lot of money for a new auditor, they usually want something in return.

In the pressure-cooker of the review program, the partners began fighting over plum accounts. They stole from one another, and backbiting and vicious office politics became the rule rather than the exception. The pressure to make more money gradually seeped into every corner of the firm. The best talent left, and a new hierarchy was established. "Grace intimidated the partners, the partners intimidated the managers and the managers were expected to intimidate the auditors," an accountant said. By 1986, the atmosphere was poisonous. It was in that atmosphere that the partners went looking for any accounts they could find.

About that time Silverado was shopping for a new accounting firm. Silverado's managers were upset with the treatment they were getting from their present auditors, Ernst & Whinney (now Ernst & Young after the merger with Arthur Young). Ernst & Whinney had presided over Silverado's financial statements for nearly a decade without much trouble. But beginning in 1982, when Silverado implemented its five-year growth plan, the firm began to spot problems. At first they were relatively minor ones that seemed to be associated with rapid growth—things like poor loan documentation. The firm dutifully noted the deficiencies and made suggestions on how Silverado could correct them. But instead of getting better, things got worse. Silverado's rapid growth didn't worry the auditors so much as the way Silverado handled it. The thrift's records were sloppy, making it difficult to get at the institution's true financial condition, and it further appeared that Silverado management didn't know what it was doing. So in 1983, Ernst & Whinney issued what is known as a "material weakness letter," pointing out that Silverado seemed to know almost nothing about the construction business, where it was lending most of its money. It also said Silverado needed to install adequate internal controls, which is accounting talk for "Clean up your act in the record-keeping department." If Silverado didn't do those things, the accountants warned, it wasn't going to be profitable very long.

The warning was to no avail. The following year, 1984, Ernst & Whinney again saw trouble. Silverado appeared to have no system at all for documenting its loans. For all intents and purposes, it looked as though Silverado were handing out money, collecting fees and commissions, then throwing some not-very- well-organized documents on a shelf, where they were all but forgotten.

These were relatively minor infractions compared with what came in 1985. Silverado managers marched in with their financial statements for the year, proudly proclaiming a $12 million profit, another record. But when the auditors began wading in, they discovered that Silverado still hadn't established a reliable system to keep track of its operations. What's more, the thrift had conjured up scores of deals that were dizzying in their complexity. Ernst & Whinney brought in outside experts to help with the audit and pressed forward. What they found raised the hair on the backs of their necks. The hundreds of loans fueling Silverado's growth over the past three years were going bad fast, a sure sign that the institution was in for heavy losses. Scheduled items, which is how bankers classify doubtful loans or loans already in default, had quadrupled. Scores of other loans were souring, too, but Silverado covered them up. Instead of letting a borrower default, the thrift set up interest reserve accounts, in which part of the loan was set aside for payments. The catch was that often, the loans weren't good at all. Silverado was, in effect, paying itself, and no money was coming in. But it looked good on the books.

For the six months the audit took, Silverado managers took turns harassing the auditors. Wise smiled and said they didn't understand the transactions. Vandapool bullied them and told them they didn't understand the transactions. But the king harasser was Bob Lewis. In a bit of irony that wasn't lost on the Ernst & Whinney auditors, Lewis had been Ernst & Whinney's partner in charge of the Silverado account until 1984, when he decided his interests were better served on the other side of the fence. While at Ernst & Whinney, Lewis had taken great joy in deriding Silverado executives, pointing out shortcomings and flaws in their financial statements. Once Lewis was on the other end of the stick, he took as much pride in harassing Ernst & Whinney auditors as he had previously taken with Silverado. "Following his move, he and I were at the center of various disputes over accounting," Herb Wulleschleger, who replaced Lewis on the Silverado account, told the House Banking Committee in May 1990. "Mr. Lewis, in his new role at Silverado, was as vigorous in his pursuit of what he apparently thought to be in the best interest of the association as he had been vigorous in his auditing at Ernst & Whinney. While he was at Silverado, my discussions with Mr. Lewis were both heated and trying."

Nonetheless, it was clear to Ernst & Whinney's auditors that Silverado was in dismal shape and that its management was going to great lengths to cover it up. So Ernst & Whinney's accountants redoubled their efforts. Instead of scrutinizing a small sampling of transactions, as is common in financial audits, they checked nearly 90 percent of them. Bad loan after bad loan surfaced, and when they were through, Ernst & Whinney auditors found nearly $40 million in loans that Silverado had neglected to account for. They discovered that Silverado's real estate-for- stock transactions, designed to make Silverado appear as though it had plentiful capital, were only so much smoke. And they found questionable "transactions with related parties," a reference to Bill Walters and Ken Good. The firm ordered Silverado to restate its earnings to show a $20 million loss and to make it clear in their financial statements to regulators that they had fallen well below regulatory standards for capital.

Silverado's managers was furious. How dare these pencil necks tell them how to run their business. There were two good reasons why Silverado's management was upset. First, a loss meant Silverado might not be able to pay dividends on its stock, which would mean preferred shareholders could take Silverado away from Wise. The second reason was money. Wise, Lewis and Vandapool had planned to collect $2 million in incentive bonuses based on the $12 million 1986 earnings. The loss Ernst & Whinney wanted them to report would have meant no bonus money.

The executives demanded to go over the heads of the Denver auditors to the home office in New York, where they hoped more sophisticated intellects would prevail. A meeting was arranged with Ernst & Whinney's brass in New York, who in so many words told them to go to hell. "Evidently frustrated with their discussions with me, management insisted on a meeting with partners in our national office, including our national director of accounting and auditing," Wulleschleger told the House Banking Committee. "That meeting did not, as Silverado's management hoped, result in a change in Ernst & Whinney's position."

That was the last straw. Silverado went shopping for a new accounting firm in June 1986, making it known it wanted people with the right judgment. Coopers & Lybrand answered the call in the person of Art Knight. Knight, a partner, was an elderly man who looked even older than he was. Years of his life had been spent clawing his way to the top of the accounting profession, and the long hours showed. He was pale and wrinkled before his time. He'd even given up his beloved cigars because of failing health. A man driven by fear, he realized that his ticket to the top was obeying orders and obeying them well. He had taken Jack Grace's review program to heart, and he was determined to make good by it. He wasn't going to sacrifice a good career, not this close to retirement.

So, hat in hand, he met with Silverado executives. They delicately asked how Coopers & Lybrand would deal with things like, well, loan losses, for example. They certainly hoped Coopers & Lybrand had more vision than that other firm. Knight replied that his firm did and that he would take some of their financial records and tell them exactly how

Coopers & Lybrand would tackle the problem. About a month later, they met again. Knight brought with him a report that Coopers & Lybrand put together to show Silverado how it would be treated. The report ignored the issue of accounting for troubled loans. (Federal regulators later said that it was a grievous omission, that the report should have concluded that troubled loans would be vigorously reported.) Silverado's executives smiled. Coopers & Lybrand was just the firm they were looking for. So, in late August, they fired Ernst & Whinney and hired Coopers & Lybrand.

Now, switching outside auditing firms is usually a serious matter and should raise all kinds of questions in the minds of federal regulators. A banking analyst in Denver said that "as an analyst, I consider that a big, big red flag. Whenever one of my companies changes accountants, I expect a very thorough, detailed explanation." But in Silverado's required filing with the Federal Home Loan Bank of Topeka, it glibly said Ernst & Whinney's fees were too high and that after nine years with the firm it was time to get some fresh blood. Silverado also said it wanted to "enhance the appearance of impartiality and independence" because Bob Lewis used to work at Ernst & Whinney. The claims, of course, were rubbish, but they were based on truth, albeit a hazy definition of it. The next assertion, however, was a bald-faced lie. It said "no disagreements had existed between Silverado and Ernst & Whinney that, if they had remained unresolved, would have resulted in a qualified opinion." An accounting firm issues a qualified opinion when it disagrees with the accounting in a financial statement. When Ernst & Whinney found out about Silverado's claim, they dashed off a scathing letter to regulators detailing nearly six months of almost constant disagreements. Morton Meyerson, the firm's spokesman in New York, put it more bluntly: "We looked at their books and said, 'Hey, you've got $38 million in bad loans here. They were going to take bonuses, but we stopped that. We saw some problems and they weren't happy about that. They got rid of us a few weeks later. Draw your own conclusions from that.'"

Coopers & Lybrand geared up to handle their new account. As is the practice on all audits, Coopers & Lybrand evaluated its expertise. It didn't seem to matter that the firm had little or no experience in auditing savings and loans, and the firm concluded its auditors were amply qualified. The Office of Thrift Supervision, reviewing the case four years later, thought otherwise. "The engagement team that was assembled lacked both the sufficient technical training and experience, including adequate knowledge of the savings and loan industry," thrift office attorneys said in their reprimand. "Coopers did not ensure that the 1986 audit was completed with the proper degree of professional skepticism as required."

Apparently, the situation was even worse than the regulators let on. The firm had put some of its least experienced auditors on the account, auditors who later admitted to being baffled by what one accountant called "the most complicated audit we've ever done." Worse, throughout the two and a half years that Coopers worked on Silverado's financial records, it haphazardly shuffled accountants in and out so that many of the accountants on the project never worked on it long enough to know what was going on.

It appeared, too, that Coopers & Lybrand didn't look favorably on its own auditors who challenged Silverado's assertions. Keith McClendon, a sharp fast-tracker who was made managing auditor on the Silverado account, saw problems in 1986. He questioned Silverado's rosy depiction of its capital and loss reserves. He was taken off the account shortly after that. Although McClendon declined to be interviewed for this book, a friend who also worked at Coopers & Lybrand said, "Silverado management had a real problem with Keith. They were saying things like, 'He's not reasonable' and 'He's not seeing things the right way.' He was fired that first year, not because he wasn't any good but because he was asking too many questions."

Despite the fact that only a year before, Ernst & Whinney had found $40 million in unreported loan losses hidden in Silverado's accounting sleights of hand, Coopers & Lybrand found nothing. In 1986, the firm said Silverado's $23 million set- aside for expected loan losses was fine. But regulators who later reviewed the same records found $35 million in additional losses. Coopers & Lybrand also allowed Silverado to inflate its capital by $14 million, making it appear healthy when it wasn't. When it was through with the 1986 audit, Coopers & Lybrand issued a glowing opinion. Regulators allege the audit was "materially misleading, reporting that Silverado was a viable institution when in fact it was materially undercapitalized."

Experts who followed the Silverado case said the rogue thrift would never have ended up such a disaster had an accounting firm been watching it closely. Abraham Briloff, an accounting professor at New York's Baruch College, said a good accountant would never have let Neil Bush get away with the transactions involving Ken Good and Bill Walters. "It is abundantly clear that the system of internal controls during that period of Mr. Bush's involvement were hideously inadequate," said Briloff, who predicted in 1985 before the Senate Subcommittee on Oversight and Investigations that accountants would be a key in an impending financial disaster. "It's my contention that none of this would have happened had there been a vigilant accounting firm on watch. While the accounting profession didn't create Silverado or any of the rest of the debacle, it couldn't have happened without its complicity. Accountants helped create the appearance of wealth when it wasn't there."

The Silverado account was the pig of pigs. But as federal authorities began shoveling through the savings and loan mess, they discovered pigs everywhere. There was a pig at Arthur Young (now Ernst & Young after merging with Ernst & Whinney) in its negligent audit of Charles Keating's Lincoln Savings. There was a pig at Touche Ross in its audit of Beverly Hills Savings and Loan. The list could go on for pages. The Big Eight had become a veritable hog farm. In

1989, the General Accounting Office ripped the accounting profession for its negligence in the thrift crisis, referring six accounting firms to federal regulators for disciplinary action. By the end of 1990, the Federal Deposit Insurance Corp. and the Resolution Trust Corp. had initiated twenty-one legal actions seeking $1.5 billion from accounting firms for alleged fraud and negligence. For its audit of Silverado, Coopers & Lybrand at the end of 1990 became the first major accounting firm in the country to be penalized by the Office of Thrift Supervision. It became a symbol of what regulators finally recognized as a nationwide phenomenon, an epidemic. "As regulators, we will pursue enforcement action against those who do not hew to the highest standards of their professions."

That such a frenzy of greed and irresponsibility should have occurred, of all places, in the accounting profession is mind- boggling. For most of their history, accountants have been bastions of conservative thinking. Almost to a fault, they adhered to a professional ethic of extraordinary objectivity. They cared for nothing but the numbers. Numbers told the truth. Everything else lied. They were the pencil-necked bean counters who couldn't hold a conversation to save their lives unless it involved cash-flow carrythroughs or amortization schedules. Of course, this image made them the subject of ridicule, as in the Monty Python sketch in which a pollster asks people on the street their opinion of the French. A bewildered-looking gentleman with a bowler hat and umbrella replies, "Well, I'm an accountant and consequently too boring to be of interest." But it was precisely that quality that helped keep the nation's businesses from running amok. In 1932, Fortune said the fact that "almost all accountants are conservative by nature, that all accountants take delight in discounting chickens before they are hatched, is what stabilizes the opinion."

But for some reason, delight for objective accounting flew out the window in the 1980s, to be replaced by delight for money. It was greed, pure and simple. But the greed didn't appear out of thin air. It was produced and nurtured by the

Reagan administration's deregulation. The accounting world wasn't directly affected by deregulation, but it was handed new rules to live by. A veteran accountant who watched with dismay what happened at Coopers & Lybrand in Denver put it this way, "Silverado paid us a hell of a lot of money," he said. "You have to understand the period this was going on. The thrifts and everybody were making so much money it was unbelievable. We saw what was going on, and we wanted a piece of the action."

Part IV

Endgames

10

The Collapse

On June 8, 1988, the inevitable happened. The Fort Worth real estate developer missed a $3 million payment on a loan from FirstRepublic Bank in Dallas, which held the first lien on the property. According to the insane terms of the original agreement, Silverado was liable for the payment, and the developer wouldn't be paying Silverado for its $74 million loan. The thrift foreclosed, just over a year after making the loan, losing more than $41 million in the process. Silverado's capital was nearly wiped out, and the thrift teetered on the brink of insolvency. The mortar that had cemented the enormous weight of Silverado's bad debt was cracking.

Other loans were going bad so fast that Sandefur wrote in January "the large number of problem assets threatens the future viability of the institution." Silverado's money desk sent interest rates higher almost by the day to keep deposits coming in. At some points, it was paying more for deposits than it was making on loans. Yet Wise told his employees and his board of directors that the slump was temporary and that Silverado would emerge to resume its path to greatness. "Up until the very last day, Mike expected to get it recapitalized," a former executive said. "He talked about it at every chance. It was a continuing posture in every meeting."

Regulators were meeting with Silverado almost weekly, imposing new sanctions and raising more questions. After one of these meetings, Wise shot back a thirty-six-page response, saying "the board has been diligent in overseeing management's activities, and although mistakes have been made, the resourceful and complex strategies utilized by Silverado to survive the difficult economic period should not be criticized because the strategies are new or different."

Meanwhile, Bob Lewis was pondering ways to get money flowing again. Regulators had ordered the thrift out of commercial real estate and into home mortgages. But they didn't say what kind of home mortgages. Since Silverado had closed most of its branch offices, it didn't have the capacity to originate enough home loans to make much difference, and besides, Lewis disdained the business. But Wall Street had devised a way to buy home mortgages without actually making the loans.

All the major firms were peddling something called Real Estate Mortgage Investment Conduits, or REMICs. A form of mortgage-backed securities, REMICs are pieces of a very large pie made up of hundreds or thousands of home mortgages. Some slices of the pie collect only interest payments, which means the security makes money when interest rates go up and homeowners cling to their mortgages. Others collect only principle, making money when interest rates go down and homeowners refinance. Profits can be enormous if you bet right on the direction of interest rates. But so can losses if you bet wrong.

Lewis bet they would fall and began picking up principle-only strips. For a while, he was right, and Silverado booked a $21 million profit—that is, until regulators took a look at the accounting. The thrift had recorded the profit according to what it thought the strips were worth instead of their true market value. Silverado reversed the profit, explaining that it had only been recorded in the first place because Coopers & Lybrand said it was okay.

But Lewis kept at it, sinking $500 million into REMICs by January. When Sandefur found out about it, he launched an

examination of the portfolio. Finding an "unhealthy concentration of assets" in REMICs and undue interest rate risk,
he ordered Silverado to stop buying the paper. It didn't. The
addict had only changed drugs. It was off heroin but making
trips to the methadone clinic.

Lewis bought more and more of the investments, buying
different portions of the mortgage pie to hedge his bets on
the direction of interest rates. The REMIC portfolio bur-
geoned to $650 million. Then interest rates went up, and the
portfolio lost $175 million.

Wise, meanwhile, scoured the country for capital and potential buyers. He realized his job was in danger. If the feds
took over, he most certainly would be the first to go. But if
he could find a buyer who would capitalize the thrift, he
could get the government off his back and keep his job.
M.D.C., the real estate company that owned $20 million in
Silverado stock, pricked up its ears and began to negotiate
for the thrift. But talks were going slowly, and Wise needed
capital—fast. At one point, he proposed a plan to raise capital
with junk bonds, which Sandefur immediately shut down.
The thrift was grasping at straws.

That didn't stop Wise from continuing to leach off the
institution, however. With the thrift crumbling around him,
Wise asked regulators to approve dividends on Silverado
stock, which he owned. The dividends Wise would have
collected would have been enough to cover a good portion
of the $1.75 million Silverado loan regulators were badgering
him to repay. Sandefur denied the request for dividends.
Wise never repaid the loan.

On June 24, the real estate appraisals van Cleave had
ordered began to trickle in. The losses hidden behind Silverado's appraisals were even bigger than the regulators had
imagined. The first two deals alone—Bill Walters projects—
showed losses of at least $21 million. Sandefur order nine
more appraisals, and by the end of July, Silverado had been
forced to recognize more than $200 million in new losses.

Silverado announced its financial condition to the public
on August 2. At a meeting in Topeka the day before, Wise

had cavalierly said he wasn't overly concerned about the impact of the announcement. Perhaps he thought his salesman's charm would prevail. In an almost gleeful press release—titled "Silverado announces first-half earnings"—Wise happily announced a $13.7 million profit "before loan loss provisions." To the uninitiated, this looked like pretty good news in a year when most of the financial institutions in the state were racking up losses. "Our earnings outlook for the balance of 1988 is also quite good," Wise said in the release. "I'm pleased by this aspect of our performance because it indicates that our game plan . . . is working well." Not until the bottom of the page, almost as a sidelight, did Silverado mention that it had lost $198 million to loan loss reserves. Not until the second page did it say anything about what it termed "a temporary negative capital position of $61.6 million."

Despite the soft-pedal, most people got the message. Silverado had just logged the biggest loss in Colorado history. It was not only insolvent, it was insolvent by a lot. The thrift owed an astonishing $100 million more than it could pay when losses from the Fort Worth loan were figured in. Both Denver newspapers ran front-page stories, and wire services sent the news around the country. Depositors flocked to the thrift, and brokers around the country were flooded with orders to pull deposits out. Silverado's money desk tried to control the panic, assuring depositors the institution was alive and well and that their money was safe in any event, protected by the full faith and credit of the U.S. government. Wise bought advertisements in newspapers with his sedate, confident smile glowing from the page. He wrote letters to publishers and influential business leaders. "It has been some time since I wrote to you about Silverado," he wrote. "The past year, to paraphrase Dickens, has been the best of times and the worst of times." He said Silverado had achieved new records in cash flow and interest margins and that remarkably low expenses had helped make the first half of the year one of Silverado's best. He danced lightly on the subject of capital.

Despite the efforts, $86 million fled the institution over the next three days. It would lose more than $100 million more by the end of the month.

On August 5, a Friday, Silverado had only $5 million left in its vaults, a pitifully small amount, especially given the skittishness of depositors. The Denver papers would be running more nasty stories over the weekend, and Wise feared a liquidity crisis of severe proportions—which, translated, meant he would have to stand behind the counter and tell depositors trying to get at their money that there wasn't any left. Silverado was bleeding to death.

For Silverado to survive, it needed money fast. And the only place it could get it was from the Home Loan Bank, which lends to institutions short on cash. Silverado had already maxed out its credit at the bank, so regulators laid down the law. If Silverado would agree to drastic regulatory action, it would lend the money.

The next day, in an emergency board meeting, Silverado accepted a consent agreement, a regulatory tourniquet that prohibited it from doing just about anything. Without permission from regulators, Silverado couldn't make loans, borrow money, invest depositors' dollars, hire employees, give raises. In effect, Silverado was under government control. But it got the money it needed. On August 7, the Federal Home Loan Bank Board in Washington authorized another $450 million in government funds to cover deposit runs at Silverado.

For the time being, Silverado had the money it needed to survive. But it was clear that the thrift wasn't long for the world when on August 15 the Colorado savings and loan commissioner issued a capital call, the first step in a government takeover. Two days later, suddenly sensitive to the appearance of conflicts of interest, Neil Bush announced his resignation from the board. "The nomination process had reached a peak," he later told government investigators. "Dad was to become the nominee for the GOP, and that obviously raises the profile of Neil Bush. At the same time, the regulators, who had been scrupulous in their scrutiny—

zealous, really—signed an operating agreement with the bank. For the playing field to be absolutely level, I thought it was important for me to be off the board. I didn't want the regulators to feel my presence on the board would have any kind of impact on their process going forward."

The truth of the matter was that Neil already was under investigation by the regulators. While sifting through Silverado's loan documents, van Cleave had discovered some fishy circumstances surrounding Silverado's dealings with Bill Walters and Ken Good. On January 27, 1987, she requested that investigators in Washington conduct what is known as a 407(M)(2) investigation into insider dealing at Silverado. As the examination wore on, a letter from Neil to Mike Wise requesting a $900,000 line of credit for Good surfaced, as did other things that looked a lot like special favors. So in September 1987, Brian McCormally told investigators in Washington to expand the probe. By 1988, the investigation was turning up some dirt—the $100,000 loan from Good, the loans from Walters' Cherry Creek National Bank and Neil's curious behavior on the board when it came to transactions involving Walters and Good.

At the time of Neil's resignation, his father was riding a crest of popularity in the 1988 presidential race, partly by painting Democratic candidate Michael Dukakis as a man whose inept policies encouraged crime. If the press—or the Dukakis campaign—had gotten hold of the fact that the Republican candidate's son was in the thick of the greatest financial scandal in the nation's history, the Bush camp surely would have been dealt a crippling blow. Dukakis would have had a field day.

No one knows whether Republicans warned Neil to get off Silverado's board for the sake of his father's presidential bid. But there were some troubling coincidences in the events that unfolded in the months between Neil's resignation and Silverado's closing December 8. Soon after the consent order and the Colorado commissioner's capital call, the bulky machinery required to shut down a thrift began to move.

All attempts to sell the institution to a private buyer had failed. Regulators dangled Silverado in front of any thrift in Colorado big enough to buy it. No one was interested. Even M.D.C., which had as much interest as anyone in keeping Silverado alive, had nosed around and smelled so much rot that it finally said no thanks. The only alternative was to close the shop. So on September 12, Terry Sandefur sent a long memo to the Federal Savings and Loan Insurance Corp. in Washington, recommending that Silverado be put in the government's hands.

A small army of examiners, lawyers and accountants began compiling the several thousand pages of documents necessary to guide the takeover through bureaucratic channels. Brian McCormally began work on a fifty-five-page "recommendation memorandum," a synopsis of Silverado's history required for government action. On October 21, the Colorado savings and loan commissioner called Mowbray in Topeka and said he would close the thrift before the end of the month.

Mowbray, suddenly and unexpectedly, ordered the proceedings to a halt. A call had come from Washington asking Mowbray to hold off closing Silverado for forty-five days. No one seemed to know why. Mowbray later explained to the House Banking Committee that the FSLIC simply put Silverado in line behind all the other thrifts it was closing. But there were holes in his story and in his memory. When the banking committee pressed him for details, Mowbray said he couldn't remember whether he or someone on his staff took the call. He couldn't remember who made the call or what reasons the caller had given for requesting the delay.

A member of his staff in Topeka had a somewhat better memory. "I remember the day very clearly," he said in 1990. "One of Kermit's assistants came up to me and said, 'Kermit just got a phone call.' He acted funny about it, so I asked him who it was. He said he couldn't tell me but that it was from Washington and it was heavy. After that, work on Silverado stopped."

George Bush was elected president on November 8. The next day, Mowbray signed the recommendation memorandum that put the wheels in motion again. The cost of that delay is in the hundreds of millions of dollars. In late September, regulators estimated the cost of Silverado's closure to be between $400 million and $600 million. When the thrift was finally closed December 9, it cost $1 billion.

The source of the call has never been revealed. An investigation was supposedly mounted by the Treasury Department in the fall of 1990. At this printing, Treasury will say only: "We don't discuss investigations, now or ever." Even if the call was completely innocent, the public may never know about it.

In the bitter cold of December 9, 1988, Silverado ceased to be. The night before, a hundred regulators— members of a special thrift takeover squad from Washington—had checked into the Writer Manor hotel across the street from Silverado under the code name Williams & Associates. The name had been drawn from a hat and had no significance, really, other than to disguise the identity and the mission.

The regulators were under strict orders not to breathe the words "Silverado," "regulator" or "takeover" while in the hotel. Under no circumstances were they to reveal their identities. If anyone asked, they were members of a marketing company in town to conduct research. No documents were to be sent or received by fax at the hotel, and nothing— not stationery, documents or notes—was to be left in hotel rooms, where a curious maid might discover what was afoot. They even took steps to avoid dressing like regulators.

They knew from experience that news of a thrift takeover could spring from the most unlikely source. The least spark could light the thirsty tinder of the rumor mill where reporters lurked, waiting to get such a story. Before they knew it, the regulators would have a catastrophe on their hands. A run on the bank could mean millions of dollars gone in a matter of hours and even violence as desperate depositors lost control. It had happened before. If word leaked, Silverado executives could also find time to destroy damning documents. No one needed to be reminded of the Navy motto: "Loose lips sink ships."

The next day, Friday, the regulators were called to a meeting. They massed in a banquet room, where they received their orders. Each member of the takeover team got a set of logistics, and the team leader, using a set of diagrams, talked strategy—points of entry, timing, security. One team would secure documents, another count cash, another oversee the transfer of deposits to a new thrift set up by the government.

When the meeting was over, only one step remained. The Federal Home Loan Bank Board was meeting in Washington. The takeover still had to be approved by the board, which acted as a financial Joint Chiefs of Staff in thrift closures. The troops were in position, but they couldn't act until word came from Washington.

The call came at 2:15 p.m. The troops would move at five. In the couple of hours before zero hour, the regulators went their separate ways, using the time to get a good meal or a nap. Finally, under a bitter gunmetal sky that produced a few feckless snowflakes, they began moving in small groups across the street. Two or three people at a time drove in rental cars, sitting in the parking lot until all had arrived. Some covered the front door, others an entrance in the rear. Other regulators were duplicating the process at Silverado branches around the city. At 5 p.m. precisely, they entered the building, showing government identification badges, locking the doors behind them and placing armed security guards at each entrance.

They moved quickly through the building to their assigned stations. Some Silverado employees were near hysterics. Many had no idea the thrift was in trouble. Sure, the papers had reported some things, but it was just talk. Wise had assured them of that. "A lot of people were under his spell," a senior vice president said. "They believed him over anything else. He said everything was fine, and people bought it. For a lot of people, the takeover was a complete shock."

But Wise apparently knew something he didn't tell his employees. He was nowhere to be found—out of town, the regulators were told. His desk and a few file drawers had been emptied. No one ever knew what documents had been taken or whether Wise had been tipped off. Some suspected the former head of the Federal Savings and Loan Insurance Corp., Stewart Root, whom Wise had befriended. The Federal Home Loan Bank Board asked the Justice Department to investigate charges that Root had given Wise advance warning. Root denied the charges. Others, however, felt certain it was Mowbray. He also denied it.

The takeover team fired Silverado's senior management, and under the watchful eye of a guard, they were allowed to pack their effects and leave. The rest of the employees were herded into a lunchroom and told what was happening to their thrift. Scores of regulators began the long, arduous task of gathering 15 million pages of documents, boxing them and preparing them for a trek to a giant warehouse, where government attorneys would spend the next two years assembling their case against the thrift. Accountants, meanwhile, erased Silverado's corporate structure and drew in a new one. In the fading light outside, workers covered the big block letters of Silverado's sign with white sheets that bore the institution's new name: Mile High Savings.

11

Exodus

A little less than a month after Silverado closed its doors, reporters were summoned to a conference room at the Westin Hotel in downtown Denver. Three or four men in suits handed out press releases while another man, older than the rest and wearing a ski sweater, sat smiling in a folding chair next to a small lectern. Presently, one of the men made a brief introduction and the older man in the sweater stood up, resting his hand on the lectern. He wore the satisfied expression of someone who'd cut a good deal for himself. Indeed he had.

The man was Robert E. Lackovic, chairman of First Nationwide Bank, a giant savings and loan subsidiary of Ford Motor Co. First Nationwide, whose only real distinction less than a year before had been installing mini banking centers in Kmart stores, was fast becoming one of the biggest savings and loans in the country by snapping up failed thrifts from the government. It was getting some sweet deals, but the one Lackovic was about to announce was one of the sweetest.

He had just bought Silverado and another Denver thrift, Columbia Savings, which had been closed by regulators earlier in the day. The two would be merged to form one $5 billion institution named Columbia after the latter thrift. It is ironic that without even trying Lackovic suddenly had what Wise had dreamed from the start: the biggest thrift in the state.

But that wasn't the reason First Nationwide's chairman was smiling. He'd bought the two savings and loans for a song, and a cheap song at that. First Nationwide put up $175 million in cash. The Federal Deposit Insurance Corp., meanwhile, peeled from its thin bankroll $1.2 billion for First Nationwide to take the thrifts off its hands. In addition to the money, the government agreed to take some of Silverado's bad loans and to protect First Nationwide against losses from the thrifts' assets for up to ten years. The package of tax breaks and interest rate guarantees the government had offered as bait in the deal would help make Columbia the most profitable thrift in Colorado the very next quarter.

The deal was part of M. Danny Wall's ill-fated Southwest plan. Wall, chairman of the Federal Home Loan Bank Board, put the plan together under increasing political pressure to do something about the savings and loan crisis. Cost estimates for the crisis were spiraling almost daily and everyone in Washington seemed to blame Wall. Wall sent armies of government negotiators to Texas, Arizona, Colorado and other states across the country to sell as many thrifts as possible before the end of the year. December 31 was more than a bench mark; after midnight on New Year's eve, tax breaks for savings and loan buyers would expire. In the frenzy, the FSLIC handed out thrifts like candy. In some cases, the buyers didn't put up any money at all. Defending his acquisition of Silverado, Lackovic said: "We're not taking advantage of anything anybody else can't take advantage of."

A few months later, First Nationwide vacated Silverado Center One, moving all its employees to Columbia's headquarters in the Denver Technological Center. The Silverado building stood like a ghost, one of the many hollow office buildings left behind by the thrift crisis. A leasing company tried in vain to rent the space vacated by the thrift, but tenants weren't interested. Finally, the leasing company changed the name from Silverado Center to Denver Centerpoint, saying that prospective tenants refused to inhabit a building with the Silverado name. One rainy day in August 1990, shortly before crews dismantled the big Silverado letters, rush-hour motorists on the Interstate that sweeps by the tower witnessed the long arc of a rainbow descending from the clouds, its colors fraying like the end of a rope as it touched the roof of the Skydeck.

Silverado's management quickly disappeared after its demise. Wise went to Wichita, Kansas, a short drive up the highway from his hometown of Emporia, where he got a job from his friend, Jack DeBoer, a self-made millionaire who had conceived the idea for Residence Inns. DeBoer rented Wise a mansion in Wichita's posh Eastbourough neighborhood, a pleasantly wooded area where streets meander between houses with single-digit addresses. A creek ambles around the property where Wise lived, and tennis courts grace the rear of the house. Wise was last reported to be looking for a home in Aspen, Colorado.

Lewis went to work for the Denver investment banking firm Newman & Associates Inc. Vandapool was hired by Broyles, Allebaugh and Davis, an advertising firm that happened to be fighting for the new Columbia Savings account. Despite the fact that Vandapool didn't have any advertising experience, Broyles made him executive vice president—and won the account.

Kermit Mowbray was fired from the Federal Home Loan Bank of Topeka in December 1988, just after Silverado's failure. He resumed his job teaching economics and finance at Peru State College in Nebraska. Mowbray told the House Banking Committee in June 1990 that he was persecuted for the systemic failure of the entire regulatory operation. "I thought I was the fall guy," he said, adding later in the hearing: "Hindsight is always twenty- twenty, as they usually say, and I probably, you know, if we knew that it was as bad as it was, different actions would have been taken."

Coopers & Lybrand quietly spirited Jack Grace out of Denver to a job in the New York office. On December 12, 1990, Coopers & Lybrand became the first major accounting firm to be punished by the Office of Thrift Supervision, which slapped it with a cease- and-desist order for its "abusive and self-serving actions." The order penalized the firm for five years, restricting its involvement with federally insured institutions and requiring it to report to regulators with the results of its audits. Arthur Knight, the partner in charge of the Silverado account, was issued a separate cease-and-desist order. Jack Grace escaped penalty. In issuing the order, thrift office director Timothy Ryan, who replaced Wall, proclaimed, "This says loud and clear that we hold accountants, lawyers and other professionals accountable for their actions, just as we do S&L directors and officers." Less than a week later, the Resolution Trust Corp. announced that it had awarded Coopers & Lybrand a lucrative contract to manage $278 million in loans and real estate formerly owned by failed savings and loans. Steven Katsanos, a spokesman for the Resolution Trust, explained: "If we refused to deal with everyone who is under some kind of question mark, we could quickly find ourselves in a position where there's nobody left to do any work."

Bill Walters defaulted on all his outstanding loans to Silverado and moved to Newport Beach, California, disappearing from the public eye until forced by subpena to appear in June 1990 before the House Banking Committee. Walters sat humbly at the witness table, fingers laced in front of him, and after a brief statement replied solemnly to questions. He didn't appear to be the evil figure the press had made him out to be. Indeed, he seemed repentant. Representative Peter Hoagland of Nebraska grilled Walters on his "moral obligation to devote your energies" to paying debts to the American taxpayer. Walters leaned forward to speak into the microphone: "The simple thing to do in a predicament of most developers in my position is to go file bankruptcy and start over the next day," he said. "I have elected not to do that. And I have elected to spend the last year and a half working diligently with my lenders, restructuring, staying alive for another day so that I can pay back every dime if I can."

Without really saying so, Walters seemed to imply that he was a financially broken man, devastated by the real estate crash in Colorado. Hoagland finally put the question to him. "Do you have any net worth left, or are you flat broke now or do you still have some assets, or what's your situation?" Again, Walters leaned forward. "Presently I would say I have a zero net worth."

Technically, zero net worth means that his debts equaled his assets, which doesn't necessarily mean he was living like a pauper. Still, the committee seemed to come away with that impression. So it was something of a national sensation when, a few weeks later, the Los Angeles Times discovered that nothing could be less true.

In fact, Walters was living a life of luxury. He and his wife, Jacqueline, lived in a $1.9 million gated estate near Newport Bay that had belonged to financier Roger Luby, a companion of John Wayne's daughter Aissa. The house had a courtyard pool and contained "richly finished furniture and lots of cut crystal," the Times said. Two Mercedes Benzes bearing Colorado plates were in the stone-lined driveway, and gardeners who said they charged the Walters $800 a month mowed the lawn.

That wasn't the half of it. Reporters and federal investigators began to find that Walters lived very well indeed. In addition to the Newport Beach house, Walters had a $1 million condominium in the exclusive Vintage Club development in Indian Wells, California, near Palm Springs, a $275,000 mobile home on a $250,000 plot of prime ocean-front property at Laguna Beach, four country club memberships and a fleet of boats and cars. He and his wife traveled to Hong Kong and attended the Macao Grand Prix.

In October 1990, Walters filed for protection from his creditors in U.S. Bankruptcy Court in Santa Ana, California. He claimed a "few hundred thousand dollars in assets," according to his lawyer, and $196 million in debts. The bankruptcy court didn't buy his story of poverty, but to its dismay, almost all Walters' wealth—including the Newport Beach house, the ocean- front property, the luxury condo, the Mercedes Benzes, a convertible Rolls Royce, a Ferrari, a Bombardier Vessel boat and property in Vail, Colorado, and Denver—had been transferred to his wife's name, out of the court's reach. A trustee for the court sued, claiming Walters purposefully hid the assets because he knew one day he'd be in trouble. At this printing, the court had succeeded only in taking two enormous gold Rolex watches, which Walters claimed were among his sole possessions. He bought a Timex to replace them, he said at a federal hearing in Santa Ana, but it stopped.

Like Walters, Ken Good appeared before Congress—his beard cut close to his chin—and told the committee his net worth was zero. Meanwhile, he too had left Denver. He spent most of his time in Tampa Palms, Florida, living in a $450,000 house, driving his maroon Maserati and commuting to a rented loft in New York's SoHo district. He had made Neil Bush a director of Gulfstream in January 1988, a job that paid $100,000 a year. And when George Bush was elected president, Good went with Neil to George's celebration. He also gave $100,000 to the Republican National Committee after claiming he was too broke to pay his Silverado debts.

In 1990, Gulfstream finally crumpled under mountains of bank and junk bond debt, and creditors took control. Good held a garage sale to unload his zebra-skin rugs and a few selected objets d'art. He put his Maserati up for sale and moved permanently to New York, where he applied to be a commodities trader. A close friend said he has controlled his gambling habit.

Good has money stored away in 174 private trusts, which contain an amount that Good claimed doesn't "come close to approaching $1 million." The trusts, however, are secret and no one but Good and his lawyer know the true amount.

The $10 million mansion in Denver, in the hands of the Federal Deposit Insurance Corp., lies empty. Shards of glass from broken skylights and windows are scattered on the marble floors. The government has been unable to sell the house, which, in the words of one government real estate specialist, is "just too much for anyone around there to afford."

Larry Mizel also disappeared from the public eye. His physician diagnosed a somewhat rare non-cancerous tumor called acoustic neuroma that arises on the cranial nerves deep in the inner ear near the brain stem. It can interfere with nerves that control hearing, sight, heartbeat and respiration but is fatal in only five percent of all cases. He was reported to be in good health, however, and afflicted only by ringing in his ears.

Still, he remained in virtual hiding through 1989 and 1990 as one investigation after another turned up shady dealings at M.D.C. The Securities and Exchange Commission forced the company to wipe out $4 million in profits it had recorded based on transactions with Silverado and others. In 1989, Touche Ross, M.D.C.'s independent accounting firm, demanded that David Mandarich resign for alleged accounting improprieties. Without admitting or denying guilt, Mandarich obeyed the order. M.D.C. hired him back as a consultant to perform the duties of president, to use the president's office and to receive the president's salary.

Shortly after the *Denver Post* broke stories about M.D.C.'s campaign money laundering, special prosecutor Bob Gallagher launched an investigation into what one investigator called the "biggest scam this state has ever seen." When the investigation was through, Gallagher had amassed 1,200 pages of evidence for indictments against M.D.C.'s top executives. But the prosecutor was powerless to do anything about it. Colorado's statute of limitations for campaign violations is just eighteen months, and time had run out. His findings were turned over to other state and federal agencies that still had time to act. But at this book goes to press, M.D.C. and company executives remained untouched by the law. And though M.D.C. shrank by almost half, it was more prosperous than it had been in years, thanks in part to a profit it booked by repurchasing its junk bonds at 60 cents on the dollar. Mizel continues to drive his white Rolls.

Construction crews broke ground at the new airport site in 1990. Walters defaulted on all his airport land loans from Silverado, and M.D.C. lost $20 million on its Silverado stock, which became worthless the moment the thrift failed. The government now owns most of the airport land left behind by the deals, and taxpayers are expected to pay in the neighborhood of $25 million to cover losses.

The Colorado attorney general began investigating land transactions between M.D.C. and Silverado at the airport site in the spring of 1991. Denver's top airport official said he believed the city had paid two to three times fair market value for airport land because it was inflated by developers. The Denver City Council questioned whether Denver even needed a new airport.

In January 1990, lawyers for the Office of Thrift Supervision summoned Neil Bush to Washington. They had already questioned him on two separate occasions. Armed with Neil's own testimony and volumes of Silverado documents, the lawyers put before him a consent agreement that would have banned him from the banking business for life. It was a moot point, Neil said later, because he didn't plan to become a bank director again. But Neil believed that the regulators misunderstood the facts and that he was being persecuted for misdeeds he didn't commit. He refused to sign. "It would have been easy for me to sign the consent agreement," he said in an interview a few months later. "But there is no basis, neither in fact nor in law, for this thing. I said, 'No way.' They were so eager in their pursuit of me that they just didn't check the facts. I decided to fight it and suffer the consequences."

So began the battle that would put his name on the front page of every major newspaper in the country and make him the living, breathing metaphor for a $500 billion debacle. By refusing to sign, he forced the government's hand, and thrift office attorneys scheduled a hearing before an administrative law judge to settle the matter. In the nine months before his case was to be heard, Neil stubbornly adhered to his belief that he hadn't done anything wrong. He never fathomed that his dealings even remotely resembled conflicts of interest and that he was placing his own gain before the safety of the institution he had sworn to protect. He staged press conferences and held interviews, explaining in logic that only he understood that his relationships with Walters and Good were "neither in fact nor appearance a conflict." He recited the words every time he made an appearance, as though repeating them often enough would convince people to believe them.

By mid summer, Neil seemed to be enjoying himself. He was "doing battle with the feds" and feeling fit for the job. In an interview, he said, "I'm drinking fruit juices and taking care of myself. I see this as a real opportunity for me." He wrapped himself in the mantle of a politician facing adversity, and he lashed out at his foes with obvious relish. At a press conference he called in June 1990, Neil adjusted his tie, swept his suit jacket back as he put his hands in his pockets and struck a rakish pose at the lectern. "Thank you all for coming," he said, his chin protruding resolutely. He denounced the media and the "self-serving regulators" who were out to get him. A reporter asked him to concede that his relationships with Walters and Good at least appeared to be a conflict. "I'll say it again," Neil snapped back, halting on each word for emphasis. His reproving glare swept the room. "There. Was. No. Conflict. Of. Interest." He looked almost like his father manhandling reporters at a White House press briefing. Indeed, he confided after one of those press conferences that politics wasn't far from his mind. The publicity had rekindled his desire to run for Congress. "I'd like to be part of a shake-up," he said. "I've seen how Congress works. I've seen how they treated me. There are some things that need to be changed. I would like to do it. It's a someday kind of thing."

But as the summer wore on, things didn't go his way. Instead of recognizing him for the hero he thought he was, people were carrying picket signs at his house, screaming, "Give it back, Neil," and radio stations were broadcasting songs, not very nice ones. In a fit of frustration, he returned a phone call from The Denver Post late one Friday night in July while celebrating his 10th wedding anniversary in Vail. For forty-five minutes, he vented. "It's a very politicized environment, and you are fueling it," he said, stopping to mention that he had shared a bottle of wine with his wife at dinner. "My frustration level has reached a peak, particularly with cartoonists and op-ed people. I'm a political football and an instrument in the crisis. The case is insignificant. It's been exaggerated and sensationalized."

By the time he appeared before an administrative law judge in September 1990, Neil was utterly defiant. He perched on the witness stand in a federal courtroom in Denver, where he slammed his fist and stamped his feet in indignation over what he called "unfair" and "outrageous" questioning from government attorneys trying to prove conflicts of interest at Silverado.

Neil wore the wounded look of a man wrongly accused, and for the first half-hour of questioning, he barely allowed thrift office attorney Stephen Hershkowitz to finish a question before crying out at the unfairness of the situation. Neil spit his words. "That's such an outrageous hypothetical, I don't think it's appropriate for me to respond," he said to Hershkowitz's question.

Neil's attorney leapt from his seat. "Your Honor, it doesn't have anything to do with this case. These are all hypotheticals."

"Is that an objection?" the judge asked.

"Yes."

"Overruled." Then, looking at Neil, his patience clearly tried, he spoke in soft, stroking tones. "Mr. Bush, I'm sorry, it's for me to determine whether it's outrageous or not. If you have an opinion . . . "

Neil interrupted, fuming. "My opinion is that it's out-rageous to speculate."

"No, no. I'm sorry. If you have an opinion with respect to the question ... "

Neil interrupted again, pouting this time. "What was the question again?"

The judge threw up his hands. Sharon, meanwhile, sat near the rear of the room, chatting gaily with court artists, asking to see their renditions of Neil.

As the hearing progressed, Neil fumed incredulously at the suggestion that he had competed with Silverado for Good's money. "That's a stretch," he said. "I mean, that's a real—I see where you're going, but the answer to—I can only very vaguely come to the same conclusion that you have." Hershkowitz stood near the witness stand, clutching a sheaf of papers. He asked the question again. "Was Gulfstream's ability to provide additional funding and investments in JNB affected by Mr. Good's ability to modify his loans at Sil-verado?"

"That's a stretch," Neil said.

"It's a possibility?"

"That's what I'm saying."

It had taken four hours of tedious questioning to extract from Neil what everyone else in the courtroom perceived as simple logic: That he had stood to gain from Ken Good's line of credit; that Walters had held him by the ears with $2 million in bank debt; that Neil might be out of a job—and a six-figure salary—if Good couldn't wriggle out of his finan-cial obligations to Silverado.

But still, he believed he'd done nothing wrong. He rationalized that Walters' investment in JNB was passive and therefore the developer didn't have any control over him. He rationalized that Good's $900,000 line of credit wouldn't benefit him because the money wouldn't go directly into his pocket. And he rationalized that his obligation to Silverado ended when he abstained from the vote to relinquish millions of personal guaranties, even though he would be receiving Good's money later. Late in the hearing, Hershkowitz asked:

"Did you ever consider whether or not you were competing (with Silverado) for funds that Mr. Good controlled or had access to?"

Neil held up his head and set his jaw. "Absolutely not."

The frightening truth of the matter is that it wasn't an act. Neil believed in his heart of hearts that he hadn't done anything wrong. Ethics expert Edward Conry concluded that "Mr. Bush does not lie. He does not actively try to conceal. He does not try to mislead. In his words, 'I mean, I can't lie and won't lie.' He became ethically myopic, unaware that his perspective or conduct were biased. He was apparently blinded even to the existence of the conflicts." That more than anything else made Neil the poster boy of the savings and loan crisis. He became a window into the board rooms of savings and loans across the country. Through him, the country saw that ethics and business ideals went out the window in the 1980s, replaced by the notion that money and importance are the birthright of a small, privileged set. To them, no crime was committed.

To the end, Silverado's executives and directors argued that their thrift was the victim of a failed economy, nothing more. If anyone was at fault, some of Silverado's executives later argued, it was regulators, accountants, lawyers and real estate appraisers, all of whom had let the thrift get away with its schemes. The real blame for Silverado's failure—like the blame for the thrift crisis itself—may never be determined because too many people, too many social forces, too many ill- conceived laws contributed to it. Government agencies—including the Federal Deposit Insurance Corp. and the U.S. Attorney's office—are trying to afix blame. The FDIC is attempting to recover $200 million from Silverado directors, including Neil Bush, in its lawsuit alleging gross negligence. Regardless of their conclusions, however, it seems certain Neil Bush will shoulder much of the blame in the eyes of the American public. He has already been elevated to a mythical status from which he can't return. He will forever symbolize the mistakes of the era.

Perhaps it is a warning, then, that soon after Silverado failed, Neil and Sharon moved to a $550,000 house in Denver's Glenmoor Country Club. Neil began another oil venture, Apex Energy, funded with a $125,000 loan from a wealthy neighbor in his new neighborhood. A spokesman for the neighbor, a cable TV executive, said Neil got the loan because the two "are good friends, obviously."

In the last of Neil's TV commentaries, filmed shortly before he resigned from Silverado, he solemnly bid his viewers goodbye, saying he was leaving TV to concentrate on business. He spoke earnestly into the camera, thanking his father and his nation for giving him the opportunity to make something of himself. "America is a great country," he concluded. "This is Neil Bush."

12

Epilogue

At 2 p.m. on April 18, 1991, a spokesman for the Office of Thrift Supervision issued a terse statement to reporters in Washington. "Finding that Neil Bush engaged in conflicts of interest while serving as a director of failed Silverado Banking Savings and Loan Association," the statement said, "Director Timothy Ryan today issued a cease and desist order against Bush."

The investigation had taken 15 months and produced 2,000 pages of depositions. The order amounted to little more than a slap on the wrist. Boiled to its essentials, Ryan's cease and desist order prohibited Bush from doing the things he shouldn't have done in the first place. It also ordered him to do things he should have done all along: Get the advice of a lawyer about the duties of a director, abstain from voting on any proposals in which he had a personal interest, make full disclosure of potential conflicts, reveal his business interests to management and the rest of the board, and "refrain generally from violating the standard governing conflicts of interst, fiduciary duties, or safe and sound operations."

The Thrift Office wasn't going easy on Neil. In fact, a cease-and-desist order—which is really designed to stop bad practices while they are still occurring—is its most stringent penalty, short of a ban from the industry. Neil was the first director ever disciplined for deeds done at a thrift he no longer worked for.

Even though he couldn't exact a severe punishment, Ryan wanted to send a message. In his order, Ryan explained: "No activity is more critical to survival and success of any insured institution than the faithful performance by its officers and directors of their fiduciary duties. By their efforts, the institution operates; only through their diligence, loyalty, care and candor may it prosper. Failure of a director to satisfy these fiduciary duties undermines the foundation on an institution's safe and sound operation. For this reason, a director's adherence to his fiduciary duties must be an obligation keenly appreciated and scrupulously followed."

The order was the least of Neil's legal problems. The Federal Deposit Insurance Corporation sued him and twelve others connected with Silverado's failure—including executive officers and outside directors—for $200 million. In its complaint, the FDIC said Neil and the other directors were "grossly negligent" in their oversight of the thrift.

Just days before this book went to press attorneys for Neil Bush and twelve other defendants in the FDIC lawsuit—including Michael Wise, Bob Lewis and Richard Vandapool—emerged from six weeks of negotiations to settle the civil suit out of court. For more than a month and a half, government attorneys grappled with the defense in secret sessions deep within the recesses of Denver's federal courthouse. They worked late most nights, drinking coffee from styrofoam cups and rummaging through reams of documents for an upper hand in the bargaining process. The talks plowed through five separate deadlines as the judge in the case, determined to reach a settlement, scheduled a new one each time talks reached an impasse.

It looked for a time as though neither side would budge. The government's case appeared solid, but the defendants were equally adamant. Their greatest defense was that blame lay in every direction. How could they be held liable when lawyers, accountants and federal regulators had gone along with their game? Indeed, Bush and other defendants dragged into the case more than two dozen outside parties—real estate appraisers, consulting firms, accountants, regulators and others, all of whom had helped or commiserated with Silverado. The Office of Thrift Supervision refused to hand over thousands of pages of documents that the defense claimed would show that regulators not only approved of Silverado's deals, but had actually encouraged them. Without any other explanation, the thrift office simply claimed confidentiality, saying it would rather accept a contempt of court citation than produce the documents. Why? Had Kermit Mobray done more damage than anybody knew about?

Up until the last week of May, 1991, it looked like the talks would fail, and the case would go to trial in October. But at the last minute, after the fourth deadline to conclude settlement negotiations had passed, lawyers commuting to Denver from Washington hammered out a tentative deal in the galley of a DC-10 between first class and coach. Four days later, late in the afternoon of May 29, 1991, after a fifth and final deadline passed, Chief U.S. District Judge Sherman Finesilver issued a terse order: "It appears the parties have reached an agreement in principle," he said. The deal was done. According to the terms of the agreement, the government would collect $49.5 million, about a quarter of the amount it sought originally and about a twentieth of the $1 billion Silverado's failure is expected to cost taxpayers.

Of the total settlement amount, $23 million came from an indemnity fund that Silverado had set up in 1986, when its insurance company refused to renew the liability policy for officers and directors of the thrift. This fund really shouldn't have been tapped as a part of the settlement since the money belonged to depositors. The FDIC had argued, in a separate case, that the fund belonged to depositors or to the federal government: "The former officers and directors are asking for what is, in effect, a preference over other creditors and depositors of Silverado Banking. Out of the potential persons most responsible for Silverado's failure, it is these same officers and directors who are arguably most culpable."

Not only did the settlement amount include the fund, Neil Bush tried to use it to pay for all of the legal bills he'd piled up, first in his fight with the thrift office and later to battle the FDIC lawsuit. "Bush is entitled to payment of expenses, including any and all attorney's fees in the defense of legal actions, claims, or proceedings made against him for wrongful acts," Neil's attorney argued. If Neil Bush is successful he won't pay a dime. Depositors would pick up his tab. Some of the other defendants will also get off without paying. Marjorie Page, one of the directors, threatened to seek bankruptcy court protection. Others could take years to pay, and perhaps even then only provide a fraction of the judgment.

After government legal fees, the indemnity fund and the potential for some defendants to avoid payment, taxpayers will be left with the bulk of Silverado's price tag.

Meanwhile, the thrift office handed over crates of Silverado documents to the Justice Department along with eleven criminal referrals. U.S. Attorney Marvin Collins of Texas took over the Silverado case from U.S. attorney Mike Norton in Denver, who had received campaign contributions from M.D.C. holdings.

The FDIC lawsuit and the looming specter of criminal charges would be by far the most severe punishments for Neil's deeds. But, in a way, Ryan's order was more significant. About the same time that Ryan issued his order, a caller telephoned the newsroom of the *Denver Post* and told me the media had missed the story about the president's son. The glint in his voice invoked an involuntary image of Deep Throat intoning cryptically from the folds of his raincoat: "Get out your notebook. There's more." I did, and for half an hour, the caller explained in a patient and articulate voice how Neil had organized the entire savings and loan crisis from a NORAD-like bunker in New Hampshire. The truth is that Neil didn't cause Silverado's failure. But in a way the whole $500 billion fiasco couldn't have happended without him. And that's what Ryan was saying in his order. *Failure to satisfy fiduciary duties undermines the foundation of safe and sound operation.* Neil's fickle adherence to ethics and duty, his belief that his own well-being came before the well-being of the institution he was supposed to serve, was the essence of the crisis. Deregulation alone couldn't have caused it. Nor could have poor oversight or a few rogue executives. The savings and loan crisis required hundreds of people who believed as Neil Bush did—directors, accountants and regulators. It required a vast abrogation of ethics that for many years have held together the machinery of capitalism, which otherwise would fly apart from the very force that drives it: greed.

Indeed, the greed that Neil came to symbolize was more than greed for money. Some say it was more destructive and that it lay at the heart not only of the savings and loan crisis, but the entire decade of the eighties. "I've been prosecuting white collar crime for more than 20 years," a government attorney told me. "Financial crimes were always driven by greed for money. But it was different this time. This was vanity. A bunch of nobodies made it big for themselves. That's what this whole thing was about."